_why wait

_why wait

*Wisdom for Life from Those
Who Have Passed Over*

CAROL MANN
JACKSON HOLE, WYOMING

contents

This book is dedicated to all those on whose shoulders we stand.

__The Plane Crash

__The First Phone Call

THE PHONE RINGS in the middle of the night only when there is something wrong. The phone next to my bed startled me awake. The voice on the other end was my brother Jeremy in California. "Carol, a plane crashed en route to Europe tonight, and I think Jonathan and Mary Lou were on that flight."

I fumbled for the remote on the night table and flipped on the television, squinting as I adjusted my eyes to focus on the harshly lit screen. CNN was already running reports of the plane crash off the coast of Nova Scotia and file tape of some of the prominent people aboard the doomed flight. There it was, previous footage of my brother Jonathan Mann, MD addressing the leaders of the world at the United Nations about the HIV/AIDS pandemic.

I realized to my horror that I had to figure out how best to let my elderly mother know. Since my father's death two years before, she was stubbornly living by herself in the big colonial house where we kids grew up in New England, and it was two hours later there. As soon as dawn approached on the East Coast, I called a dear friend who I knew was an early riser. Without a moment's hesitation, she agreed to go immediately to my mother's house and be there with my mother when I called with the sad news.

It was daylight in Wyoming, where I live, when the official announcement came that there were no survivors. My brother and his wife and more than two hundred men, women and children from all over the world perished in the sea off the coast of Halifax, Nova Scotia. The date was September 2, 1998.

The aftermath of the tragedy was an extraordinary unfolding of events. I had never experienced so much grief and shock and love at the same time. Knowing that surviving family members needed to be at the crash site, the airlines immediately stepped in and arranged transportation, lodging and escort service for everyone involved. We traveled to Nova Scotia right away and were treated with dignity and human kindness beyond what might have been the required protocol.

A small caravan of chartered buses ferried the hundreds of family members who had hastily flown in from all over the globe to a military base outside of Halifax, where the retrieved wreckage, cargo and scattered personal belongings were arriving in a sad, steady stream. We were asked to file alongside all they had thus far collected and to identify anything we recognized. One of the most surreal and eerie items on display was a collection of watches pulled from the ocean, which were still ticking. I was relieved that nothing there that day belonged to Jonathan or his wife.

After that ordeal, which also included someone from every family giving a blood sample for future DNA identification of the dead, the next destination was the crash site by the ocean.

What touched me most was the love and compassion from total strangers at the crash site in Nova Scotia. Schoolchildren heaped us with hand-drawn cards, and teddy bears were handed out to our children. It was damp and cold, and the sea was rough. Volunteers handed us blankets to put around our shoulders. Other kind hearts gave us food. Even the ever-present news reporters were quiet and respectful that day.

The Royal Canadian Mounted Police formed an honor guard, a human chain, down the steep rocks to the sea. Each of us was invited to take a rose, hand it to the first man in the chain and tell him the name of our loved one. He then spoke the name out loud and passed the rose to the next person in the honor guard, who did the same, until the man closest to the water recited the name for the last time and tossed the rose into the sea to be carried away with the tide. Grief is like the tide; it would crash over me and then recede over and over for many months to come.

In the midst of it all, I found myself listening with interest to people's reactions to the crash. Many were going down the path of anger and blaming the accident on the pilots as a way to cope and perhaps to ease their pain. It was clear that everyone who lost someone on that plane, including me, had to make an important choice. I could go down the path of blaming and being angry, which would close my heart. Or, I could keep my heart open, feel the pain and the love, and see where that path would take me. In that moment of awareness, I chose the latter.

_The Second Phone Call

Several weeks later, I had a second life-changing phone call related to the plane crash. This time it was during the day and not at all an emergency. My friend Tara, who is very intuitive, couldn't wait to give me a simple suggestion. "Carol," she burst out in an excited voice, "you have been working with people doing clairvoyant Soul Readings for decades. You are clairvoyant. Why don't you use your gift to communicate with your brother Jonathan, and who knows, maybe also with other souls no longer with us."

This is what I call a blind flash of the obvious. I had never considered doing this. I tried it right away. Centering myself, I became very still and said Jonathan's name silently in my mind. There was an immediate heart connection. I heard his voice and wrote his words.

For me there was profound comfort in communicating with my brother and knowing he was okay. I was also very excited to learn "firsthand" information about life after death, and to experience that souls on the other side are as eager to communicate with us as we are with them.

"The gory details are disturbing to you...
you will learn them all eventually, but I assure you,
I felt no physical pain at all."

*–*Jonathan

___The First Transmission from My Brother

This was the first Transmission from my brother Jonathan Mann, MD after he perished in the plane crash in 1998. It was later revealed by air traffic control in Halifax, Nova Scotia, that there had been fifteen minutes between the time of the first SOS from the passenger jet to the time it crashed, killing all on board. In addition to this first Transmission from my brother, Chapter 9 is devoted to his communications to me from the other side.

Dear Carol,

It is true that I am impatient and eager to be in touch with you. It is so very reassuring and fulfilling for me that you can enable communication between our different realities.

First of all, this was not what I expected...what I mean is, I never expected to die young...(ha, ha, I know I was in my early fifties and "young" is a matter of perspective).

It was a normal plane flight, and we had settled in for a long trip. There was no indication of any trouble till they took back the dinner trays and made an announcement of some mechanical difficulties. They said we'd be making an unscheduled landing in Halifax.

Here were some of my first thoughts: Concern, but

no panic, no unusual noises. The cabin lights turned off…
figured the problem is electrical…not life-threatening…
we could fly all the way to Europe without good lights
in the cabin.

Then we started to wonder if it was serious. We
could not tell if the plane was flying low or in circles. It
was dark out, the weather good, and we were not far
from shore. "At least we're not over the mid-Atlantic," I
thought or mumbled out loud.

Mary Lou and I held hands and smiled at each other
with mutual attempts at reassuring the other. We have
both been on too many planes in our lives to get too upset
right away. When we were told to take off our shoes and
any sharp objects in case we needed to prepare for a
water evacuation…we knew. Our hearts sank. Oh God.

I was sad if this is how we exit…not so much the
how, but the now. Why now, when things were so good
in our lives? Maybe I said these thoughts out loud: "Don't
we get to enjoy it, or does one just get to the happiness
and then it is gone? Maybe people stave off happiness to
keep death at a distance?"

We spoke to each other of our deep love and gratitude for having met each other and that if worse came
to worse, at least we were together. We held each other
very tight sitting in this surreal suspension of time. Our
bodies screamed silently in the imminent danger.

My senses scanned for data, still listening for
word from the crew, looking out the window, but there
was nothing to see. I silently recited a prayer; it was
instinctive, a way to ask for help. Where's Halifax
already? Suddenly there was calm in the "eye of this

storm"...acceptance.

Please know that the moment of dying is not a difficult experience. It occurs in a seamless way. There is no physical pain, regardless of what is happening to the body. The gory details are disturbing to you...you will learn them all eventually, but I assure you, I felt no pain at all. I witnessed what happened, but not from inside my body.

There was no sensation in the plane of up or down or moving in any direction. The cabin was dark, and it was nighttime outside. I don't know that I can separate what I perceived while I was still alive from what I experienced being out of my body. I do recall the sounds of screaming and an awful bang, and then silence.

And then, there we all were. Everyone who had been on the flight was hovering over the ocean looking down at this huge sinking mass of metal and debris. We were observers to the mess...everything bobbing and floating and starting to sink...hot and cold. Somehow we could see it all even though it was dark out.

We all had to conclude, even though it seemed unreal, that we must be dead. No one was crying anymore or in pain. It was as if we were all shaking ourselves after a fall, making sure we were all still intact. No one was even talking; it was more like collective disbelief. We were all somehow aware of looking at this chaos below us and trying to comprehend what it all meant.

Thoughts and feelings raced through me with such speed that there was no chance to ponder anything for long. I had passing thoughts of annoyance...okay, I was pissed...about a bunch of things. First was that I never expected to die this way or at this time. There were so many unfinished things in my life. I was worried about my three kids. I wouldn't be at their weddings, and I would be cheated out of the chance to enjoy grandchildren.

There was too much loss to comprehend. Thoughts rushed by like the wind. It was impossible to hold on to any single thought or feeling. They would disappear as fast as they came in. Somewhere in there I was upset that I had no preparation for this; I had no opportunity to share final thoughts, feelings, and love with all of you after a lifetime of closeness and shared history. Lastly, I had a bit of self-pity. Here I was, so looking forward to slowing down in my life and working less and then...boom!

It was confusing to try to hold on to the familiar reality of being alive as a way to make sense of everything. Where are we? What are we experiencing? If this is dead, then dead is not what we think. Trying to understand this while my recent life was receding like an echo was very challenging. I was trying to grasp the new reality and keep hold of my familiar self, so I could figure it out before it changed again.

There were other things going on, as well. I was trying to see if Mary Lou was with me and if we looked the same. There were people approaching...at least I assumed they were people. They looked like a blob of light coming toward us...greeting all of us passengers, all at once. Specific individuals seemed to emerge and then approach each of us. It was something like the scene when you arrive at an airport.

"Who is coming for me? Where is Mary Lou?" I wondered. I somehow knew her dad was there. "That's

good," I noted to myself. Our Aunt Betty differentiated from the collective and manifested before me. I have not seen her in decades and yet she appeared exactly as I would recognize her. I instantly felt loved and safe.

Like welcomed visitors, we were being offered comfort and enough recognition to feel okay. How does this work? Here is what I began to understand. People's souls are part of a collective, nonindividuated state of consciousness, which also has the ability to individuate in a split second when called by someone they once loved.

I think this is how the undifferentiated "crowd of people" who initially approached us then became distinct individuals when they interacted with us. I suspected that, in the timeless experience before the crash, everyone's mind must have done an automatic, unconscious "Internet search," a "calling out" for deceased friends and relatives.

Some other friends and colleagues of mine, adults and children alike, greeted me. They were all people who had been a part of my life in mutually caring ways. These were not all relatives or even friends; some were former patients and some were people I had not even been in touch with for decades. Yet, there was the pleasure of mutual recognition. The sensation was that I was part of their lives and they were part of mine. I figured I had somehow conjured them to me now, and then I felt sure that everyone was being equally taken care of. I relaxed into the experience.

I have so many questions I need answered about life and death. You know how my curious mind works, and I want to share the answers I discover with you, so I will *be telling you more next time we "talk."*

As for you, please do have the courage to keep writing letters dictated from the other side. I will be glad to help you in any way that I can. If you are willing, you might make yourself available to others who lost loved ones on this flight. I think you will find there is quite a backlog of messages.

Also, know that even though what you receive is not verifiable, you can trust that the general understandings are all true.

Love, Jonathan

The death of a loved one always leaves the living suffering from the grief of their loss, and fear of the unknown. What I have learned is that when people die, the personality quickly fades, giving the soul center stage. Just as in the current technological world, as the "Cloud" stores all our computer data, our souls contain the records of all our life experiences and everything we have learned. This treasure trove of information makes souls on the other side an untapped resource for knowledge and wisdom, helping us to live more fulfilling lives. The inspiration for this book is to bring you direct Transmissions of wisdom and advice from the souls of people of all ages who are no longer alive.

For the past decade, I have had the privilege of using my psychic talents to access insight and information about life, death, and beyond for clients whose loved ones have passed over. I have learned how people no longer alive, in our understanding of that word, are very much aware and are truly eager to communicate with us. They want to let us know about the experience of dying to allay our fears, to open our minds, to broaden our horizons and to heal our hearts.

I have discovered that what we call "the other side" is a far less limited reality than ours, and they have access to more objective and larger perspectives about so many things…not to mention that knowing our consciousness survives the death of our physical bodies is a huge relief from fear and a healing from loss.

I have organized this book to not only share my personal story, but to share the stories of others I've worked with over the years, both living and no longer alive. I have grouped the Transmissions in chapters pertaining to age, relationship, and individual circumstances; ending with a beautiful conversation from a woman on the brink of death, who was able to communicate from this side and the other side. Each chapter concludes with "Pearls of Wisdom" from the Transmissions and a "Why Wait Meditation" that is designed to bring inner peace and greater fulfillment to our lives right now.

Hopefully, like me, you are inspired by what those on the other side have to say, as their wisdom applies to us all. May this serve as an invitation to expand our hearts and minds, to learn from their insight and apply it to upgrade the quality of our lives.

Introduction

__My Story

I WAS BORN CURIOUS to know what is really going on in this world and began asking a lot of questions early on. With total uncensored abandon, I would ask my parents about whatever curiosity I was playing with in my mind. Of course, I always assumed they would know the answers.

Thankfully, while my father and mother were entertained by my imagination, they enjoyed that I wanted to learn. My father answered my questions with his own special balance of child-appropriate facts and gentle teasing.

For example, our family would spend part of the summer at the ocean when I was a young child. The mystery of the tides captured my wonderment, and I remember asking my dad, "Why do the tides go in and out?" He told me a simplified bit of truth about tides and the moon, and then with a huge grin lighting up his face, he continued by telling me that there was a giant plug in the middle of the ocean, like the plug in our bathtub at home. Every morning he'd go out in the ocean and pull the plug so the tides would go out, and at the end of the day he'd go out again put the plug back in place so the tides would fill up again.

Needless to say, I remember his story more than the facts he shared, even though I also took secret pride in thinking I could never be fooled.

When I was in first grade, I had a very short stint in Sunday school because I was always asking questions, which somehow offended my teacher. Likely I was also being a pest in class. Not far into the school year, we were learning about the story of Noah and the flood. My hand shot up like a rocket when the teacher read from the Old Testament where it said that Noah was hundreds of years old and his wife was equally old when they had a baby.

My dad was a physician, and I knew some of the facts of life. I wiggled in my seat with the excitement of revealing my knowledge and the impatience of having to wait my turn. When my teacher acknowledged me, I asked, "How was that even possible, first of all, to live hundreds of years and then to have a baby, being that old?" I followed with wondering out loud if they counted differently thousands of years ago or if they really lived that long.

The teacher paused, and I assumed she was considering her answer to a really good question. It shocked me when she broke her silence, pursed her lips and replied, "Carol, leave the room and stand outside the door until I call you back in." I had no idea why this was happening, but of course I obeyed and stood crying until she came to get me at the end of class.

At home, my parents offered a supportive explanation by suggesting that perhaps my question might have upset the teacher because she didn't know the answer. All I could grasp at the time was that the teacher was mean, she had shamed me in public, and I did not want to ever go back to her class.

I did return for some more Sundays because my parents convinced me that I would feel better about myself if I did not give up. I gave it a try, but I had lost interest. I kept any further questions to myself and was miserable. Thankfully, seeing my spirits plummet, my parents allowed me to quit.

My passion for discovering the truth had made me vulnerable, and I had crumbled with the teacher's disapproval of my authentic curiosity. Unbeknownst to me at the time, this childhood experience had set the stage both for the unfolding of my life's work and for the path of my personal growth.

I would continue learning and thinking outside the box. Eventually, I would explore the frontiers of human consciousness and devote my work toward revealing more of our true human potential. I would also have to learn to trust my "inner knowing" and to not shut down when others did not validate my perspectives.

And thus, my natural talent for seeking answers to the deeper mysteries of life became perfectly paired with my personal life lesson, mastering the skill of self-validation. I could not fulfill one without the other. This is part of the mystery and the design perfection of my life.

___Was I Clairvoyant as a Child?

People often ask if I was clairvoyant as a child. The answer is not a simple yes or no. My earliest childhood interests and curiosities were always about what was beyond the five senses. However, no one in my family ever named, confirmed, or overtly supported my intuitive gifts. For many years, I was loved, happy, and creative without a clue that I saw things differently from others.

At age six and with great pride, I announced that I traveled to other lands at night. "That was an interesting dream you had," my parents chimed in unison. "This was not about dreaming," I would insist adamantly. Leaving my physical body in my bed and going elsewhere at night was a routine experience for me. "Most of the time," I recall gushing with unabashed enthusiasm, "I visit and learn from someone I love who's very wise and lives in another place. I call her 'The Lady.'" I would literally shiver with excitement to share these intuitions and my nighttime journeys with my parents. "Carol, you have a great imagination," was always the amused reply.

Convinced that everyone could fly, I told my younger brothers I would teach them. They loved this idea. I confess this turned more into a way of manipulating my brothers to be nice to me, but my nightly experiences leaving my body made me certain that the ability to do this was real and could be taught.

One of the first books I can remember reading on my own in elementary school was a story, which I loved, about the end of the Neanderthal cavemen and the emergence of the Cro-Magnons. Even then I wondered about how we would also evolve and be replaced by another more advanced human race. After devouring children's astronomy books, I was both curious and concerned about what would happen in several hundred million years when our sun would burn out.

In retrospect, there was a common theme in all my early interests. I was seeking out the records of life on Earth. One track was the natural world in fossils, rocks, and the outdoors. Another was uncovering the records of human evolution. A third was pondering the connection between the Earth and the stars and the likelihood of other forms of higher intelligence.

It took many decades of following my calling no matter where it led, to validate that I had an intuitive gift and, therefore, was able to see and to know things beyond the physical world. It also took time to discover that by using my psychic abilities I could access the records contained in a person's soul.

This was like having an admission card to the most interesting and extensive library imaginable. In the seemingly infinite hall of records in every person's soul, I could begin to satisfy my passion to know the deeper truths about who we are, why we are here and how we could maximize our personal and collective human potential.

Now back to the initial question, "Was I clairvoyant as a child?" My answer is that we all have our soulful gifts right from the beginning and naturally they flourish most easily when they are recognized and supported early in life.

Therefore, when my daughter was about four years old and spontaneously started talking about having been on the Titanic and describing her stateroom on the ship in great detail, I knew this was a past life memory and not her imagination. I take the greatest joy in being the kind of parent who could validate her then, as I continue to do now, encouraging her to share and to further develop the gifts of her soul.

____Discovering Reincarnation

I went to the newer of the two high schools in the town where I grew up. Some of the advanced foreign language classes were only held at the older school across town and a bus would ferry us there each afternoon for last period. I always grabbed a window seat on the bus for the chance to look out and daydream.

One day, while en route to our class at the old high school, an elderly man suddenly stepped in front of the bus, like a deer jumping out of the woods. This happened at a busy intersection near the town library. The bus lurched as the driver tried to avoid the inevitable, tragic collision.

Since there were no seat belts in those days, we also slid around and off our seats with the zigzag of the vehicle. The bus came to a screeching halt and traffic stopped. While we got ourselves repositioned and checked to see that everyone on the bus was okay, people outside gathered around the man who was sprawled face up on the pavement.

Peering out the bus window at my seat, I saw the man's ashen, bluish-tinted face with his smashed eyeglasses lying next to him, and I knew he was dead. I had never seen a dead person, and this shook me to the core.

Mixed in with feelings of horror and unconsciously rubbing together my instantly cold, sweaty palms, I had a flash of sudden insight: I just knew that the body lying on the street was not the same as the man who had been living moments earlier with his own personality and unique life story.

Whatever had been animating that person was gone. The body lying in the street now was just flesh and bones. I didn't mean to be disrespectful, but his body seemed like a piece of meat compared to the person he was a few minutes before.

The ambulance came; the man was put on a stretcher and covered head to toe with a sheet. After all the police formalities, the bus drove on and dropped us off at our class. Our teacher gave everyone who had been on the bus ample time to tell the other half of our classmates from the old high school what happened on the way to class. Even though there was no such thing as formal crisis intervention training at that time, Miss Waters must have had great instincts because she gave our half of the group an in-class assignment to write about our experience.

That essay gave me the opportunity to unravel more of the experience I had witnessed and to gather my insights. I thought out loud on paper about how everything in nature is recycled every season, how our bodies are made up of the same natural elements, which are recycled back into the Earth. The next part of my logic was to assume that the living essence of the person...their soul, which I had just observed leaves the body at death, also must recycle. It just made sense.

I had no idea this was called reincarnation, or that there were thousands of years of wisdom and written teachings in many of the world traditions on this topic. No one in my family or any of my teachers had ever mentioned the subject.

However, what I took away from the out-of-the-ordinary event riding the bus to our final class period that day was a seminal experience. I knew there was more to this thing called life and death, and a passion to explore the mind-expanding possibilities was ignited within me.

___Developing My Practice

Like two intertwining spirals, my life-long love of things spiritual and the study of metaphysics were never far from my more traditional career roles in higher education, the high-tech industry, and entrepreneurship. As I was thoroughly contributing to and growing from each of my careers, I was also moving in the direction of sharing the knowledge of things spiritual and my clairvoyant gifts as a full-time career.

One of those stepping stones happened early on during the years I was teaching college-level Behavioral Science courses in the '70s. The academic climate was just right at that time for me to propose teaching a first-ever course on Psychic Discoveries in the college's Evening Division, which thankfully became very popular. The same year, a fellow professor offered to teach me hypnosis. With that new skill in my repertoire, I launched into experimenting with past life regression several decades before it became more mainstream. On weekends and evenings, my trusting friends allowed me to guide them back to past lives. We were all fascinated by the doors this opened to explore a whole other realm of who we are. Equally exciting was uncovering historical information reported during the regressions, which could later be validated. Remember, I was the child who wanted to know the untold parts of history and who we are, and in a sense, this was eyewitness information.

I moved from academia to the high-tech industry in the early '80s when there was a burgeoning interest in, and funding for, employee training programs in management skills and personal growth and development. As Corporate Training Manager in a worldwide corporation, I was responsible for an entire curriculum of nontechnical courses offered to employees in the company. I loved this position. It was like running a mini-college inside the high-tech company. Occasionally, I would also teach my favorite personal growth and development courses. The programs were very well received and as the number of alumni grew, I began noticing that more and more people coming to my office with legitimate business agendas would linger longer to also share their intuitive experiences. In those days, talking openly about dreams, premonitions, and other ESP phenomena were not common topics of conversation, and most certainly not in the business world. My office in "Corporate America" became fondly known as "The Cosmic Café," which eventually became the name of my business.

I was married during the years I was working in the high-tech industry, and my husband owned a rapidly growing design firm. He would come home after a day interviewing potential new employees, frustrated that the information in those conversations had become a confusing blur in his mind. As he said, "Most people can talk a good game." Without telling me anything about the names on his final list of candidates, he asked me to help him by clairvoyantly "tuning in" to each of the names before he'd call them back for a second interview. He was hoping I could access further insight into their character and skill sets, helping him cull the truly talented and honest people. I welcomed the opportunity; here was a new, practical application for my gift. Based on what I gleaned about each person on his list, he was then able to direct his second interview to determine if the information I accessed was valid. The insightful psychic input became an extremely helpful adjunct to the hiring process by streamlining the interview process and selecting better employees.

It didn't take me long to experiment with going deeper than someone's job qualifications. As I honed my intuitive abilities, I discovered it was possible to clairvoyantly access the records of a person's soul just from knowing their name. I discovered that unexplained fears, natural skills and talents, current challenges and behavior patterns seemed to have their genesis in the soul's past life experiences, which then carry forward for better and for worse into this life. Therefore, I reasoned, gifts and talents could be further developed in the here and now. Negative patterns of thought and behavior could be dismantled for the opportunity to evolve beyond their limitations. I was eager to know if soul-based knowledge could be applied to accelerate the healing processes in therapy. I had to find a way to test this on real clients and their therapists.

Since life always provides wonderful synchronicities, many of my friends at the time were very open-minded psychotherapists. They allowed me to offer complimentary, tape-recorded Soul Readings to selected clients who were open to the idea. The clients would share the recording with their therapists. The two would then use the information in their work together and give me feedback. I did this for an entire year, gaining confidence from receiving consistently positive responses on how the Soul Readings "connected the dots" to previously unanswered pieces of that person's puzzle. The soul-based information was deemed spot-on and extremely helpful, often cathartic in their healing work together. This gave me the confidence to charge a fee for my Soul Readings and to move one step closer to a metaphysical career, but not quite yet; I still did this work on the side.

Fast forward to the late '80s when my husband, our daughter, and I had moved to the West where we co-owned and co-managed a ski resort in the Rockies. One brisk winter morning before heading to my office at the resort, I stood as usual brushing my teeth while enjoying the magical view of the snow-covered mountain peaks glistening in the sun. Out of the blue, I had an OMG moment. The words in my head were, "The time is now." I realized immediately that meant the time had come to step fully into my spiritual work and to share it. The accompanying epiphany was that just because I was competent at management didn't mean I had to do it for the rest of my life. Searching for a more mundane example to shore up my insight, I mused out loud with a giggle, "Just because you are good at cleaning floors does not mean that it's yours to do." Resigning from my management job at the resort and quitting the successes of the high-powered work world cold turkey was something like traveling at a very high speed and suddenly coming to a halt. It was a painful transition and identity shift, and it took many months to regain my new momentum.

In all the years since, I have created a career dedicated to sharing the wisdom in our souls by offering clairvoyant Soul Readings, facilitating workshops, and teaching seminars nationally and around the world. In the year 2000, I began producing a local radio program on topics where science and mysticism meet, called of course, "The Cosmic Café." My menu of services is for people of all ages who are eager to expand their hearts and minds by learning more about who they are, knowing their life's purpose and seizing the opportunity to ride the wave of evolution, which beckons us now. I am forever grateful for every step along the path and have never looked back.

When my brother died his untimely death in a commercial plane crash more than a decade ago, I began applying my clairvoyant gift to communicate with his soul. In the years since, I have also been able to serve as a messenger for clients whose loved ones have passed. I receive the communications from people no longer alive in the form of letters, which I call Transmissions. All the

Transmissions in this book are actual messages from real people of all ages. I have only changed their names. Some of my clients have generously volunteered to introduce the Transmission they received through me from their loved one so you can benefit from the added dimension of their personal experiences. Other Transmissions stand on their own for you to glean their messages.

___How I Do This Work

Communing with souls who have passed over and then sharing the communication with their living relatives or friends is a gift, an extraordinary collaboration, and challenging work.

The first step is accessing the soul of the person who is no longer alive. I need three facts in order to do this: their name, the cause of death, and the relationship to the client. I then make myself very still and say the name of the deceased person silently in my mind. Almost immediately the connection with their soul is established. I fondly call this process my "Cosmic Google."

The communication I receive is hard to describe because it is a combination of words, images, feelings, and symbols all rolled into one. I call it a "thought ball"; however, it is more accurate to say it is a hologram. I then sort out the multisensory information, sit at the computer and translate it into words.

As translator of the hologram, I do my best to reflect the person's syntax and to always maintain their intent and meaning. At the same time, it is inevitable that some of the words I use to clarify their concepts, as well as how I organize the content, can reflect my editorial choices.

I have discovered that using the format of a letter is the most personal and also facilitates my process. As soon as I write, "Dear so and so," the rest of the message in the "thought ball" unravels into distinct themes and begins to flow with ease. Sometimes I sense that I haven't gotten it quite right. In that case, the person on the other side urges me to add, subtract, or change something I have written.

The first thing people want to know is that their loved one is okay and not in pain. Thankfully, every soul immediately confirms that they are fine. As I am communing with the person on the other side, I experience a vivid sense of them in the life just completed. Those perceptions often include their brand of humor, their passions, their guiding principles and some of their sensitivities.

There are a couple of things that can be challenging for the living. First, as you will see, the person on the other side is very happy where they are. Their exuberance is not ever intended as a slight to the living, but if it is interpreted that way, it can feel hurtful to the person grieving the loss. Secondly, although people know in advance that communications from the soul are not sentimental, it can be disappointing that the Transmission is not romantic or highly emotional.

The common message in all the Transmissions is that love prevails. The bottom line of the soul is love. This truth offers the best reason to drop the small stuff in our daily lives and to reap the joy of coming from love while we are here.

___Reincarnation and the Transmissions in This Book

When I do Transmissions, I have no idea what the person will choose to share. This makes it extra interesting when certain ideas come through again and again. A recurring theme in many of the Transmissions in this book is that sometime in the future the soul will be incarnating in another human life on Earth.

Here is some brief information about reincarnation that I hope gives you a context in which to better understand what these Transmissions are suggesting when they refer to future lives.

For thousands of years, most of the world's religions, indigenous traditions, and esoteric teachings have espoused the idea that consciousness survives the death of the body, and the soul reincarnates in subsequent lives to continue its journey of learning and contribution.

A surprising fact to most Westerners is that there are more cultures in the world today incorporating the idea of reincarnation than those who do not. Reincarnation is a relatively new concept in the West, although a short list of notable world figures that have publicly embraced reincarnation includes Aristotle, Shakespeare, Benjamin Franklin, Carl Jung, Thomas Edison, Henry Ford, and General George S. Patton. The latter actually used, by his own admission, military strategies in his desert campaigns, which he recalled from a past life as a general in the Roman Army.

For the past forty years or so, there has been significant research in the effort to prove the reality of conscious life after death. Right now we have many ways to glimpse that possibility, but no scientific proof.

One glimpse is the now well-known phenomenon of the Near Death Experience, in which someone who is pronounced medically dead miraculously revives and is able to share accurate details about conversations and activities that took place during the time they were totally unresponsive. There are tens of thousands of recorded cases of the Near Death Experience from children and adults worldwide.

One recent and outstanding example is the experience of an American neurosurgeon who was in a coma for a week. Doctors monitored him closely the entire seven days. The cortex of his brain was completely shut down, making him brain dead. Previously a skeptic, when this physician unexpectedly awoke from the coma, he shared life-changing experiences of a world beyond our brains and our bodies where death is not the end of our consciousness.

Another view is Past Life Therapy, in which professionally trained therapists successfully use hypnosis to regress people back to a time before they were born to uncover the past life origins of current, unexplained emotional or physical issues. When the source of trauma was in a prior life, there is a powerful catharsis and often the complete resolution of the issue.

One more source of information is the many cases of young children who are able to recall specific details of their prior lifetimes. Fortunately, parents of these children have brought this to the attention of professional researchers who have validated and documented the historical accuracy of information provided by the children.

Psychics can also tap into a client's previous lives. Please note that what someone tells you must resonate deeply within and truly make sense to you for it to be valid. When past life information rings true, it offers profound insight for the client into current-day interests, aversions, strengths, and weaknesses. This is always healing and useful, even in the absence of hard scientific proof.

There is no need to embrace the concept of many lives; we will all discover whether or not this is true someday. Right now, you are invited to enjoy all the information and wisdom in these letters from the other side with a curious mind and an open heart.

___Personal Insights

In the process of choosing what to include in this book, I am rereading more than a decade's worth of Transmissions for the first time. This is unexpectedly giving me the special gift of self-reflection. When I am working, my focus is appropriately on the communication with the person no longer alive and then with the client. Re-reading the Transmissions, I am inspired to reflect on my own experience and the many gifts I have taken away from doing this work.

I am struck by the wealth of universal truths in these letters. Each letter has so many important messages for living well here and now. Though the letters were directed to a specific person, the teachings about living well are applicable for everyone.

I keep checking in to see if I have evolved in some of the ways suggested by those on the other side. Do I drop the small stuff? Do I live with gratitude and focus on what is right in my life? Do I live from the glass-half-full perspective? Do I see the miracle in all of Creation? Do I consciously choose love over fear? I can say the answer to these questions is, "Yes, most of the time." Reading the letters reminds me to continue being mindful of the many truths shared in these pages and to get back on track with myself as gracefully as possible when I forget.

Certainly, I have become more comfortable with death. Without the drag on my system from that background fear, I notice there is much more energy for living.

It is bittersweet to recall that I would never have added this work to my repertoire had my brother and his wife not perished in the crash of Swissair #111 in 1998. As I have been writing I have been aware of Jonathan's presence.

I had not initially thought of including my deceased parents in these pages. The inspiration to write about my mother was the result of a homework assignment when I was in a recent class for writers. It was another blind flash of the obvious that I could ask for a Transmission from her. What she shared was endearing and healing for me. I had not planned to include anything from my dad until it was clear to introduce his wisdom in the Afterword of the book. This makes me smile because he loved to have the last word in conversations.

I have brought my parents back into my life in a new way with their Transmissions. Though they were not great fans of the paranormal realm, I can once again enjoy and benefit from the wisdom of their souls. What they have shared moves and inspires me.

Another realization is that this book is a remarkable and unusual collaboration with the people who entrusted me to do these Transmissions and those no longer alive who have shared their experiences and insights so graciously. I have only known a few of these souls "in person."

I am also appreciating something about myself for the first time: It takes courage to be a pioneer, regardless of the arena. Of course I know this as a concept, but I am feeling it in relation to what I do.

It is a blessing to have this gift of clairvoyance, which allows me to access the wisdom in a person's soul, whether they are living or they have passed over. It is a privilege to interact with people at this deep level.

In this work, I put myself out on a long limb since there are two aspects requiring a big leap of faith. The first is whether the personal reflections of the deceased, expressed in the Transmission, will resonate to their living relative. The second is there is no concrete proof as yet for the part of the Transmissions that describes what happens at the time of death and beyond.

It comes as no surprise to remind myself, once again, that trust and self-validation are two things I am intending to master in my life this time around. I am in awe realizing how I've chosen content like these Transmissions and Soul Readings for the living, which pushes me to grow personally at the same time that I am also helping others.

I suspect this is how it is intended to work for everyone: Contributing the gifts we are given will naturally provide the fertile ground for our own personal evolution.

___Jonathan Introduces My Book

As I began to formulate this book, I asked my late brother, Dr. Jonathan Mann, if he would like to contribute by "writing" his own introduction. Here is his Transmission:

Dear Readers,

Letter writing has always afforded a way to share intimate feelings, deep thoughts, and personal perspectives. Sometimes, allowing the flow of spontaneous thoughts on a page also brings forth unplanned truths and inspiration. As with regular letter writers, those of us who are no longer living among you have the opportunity to share things that might have been neglected or too difficult to broach in person.

We also benefit from the fact that our personalities (egos) are significantly diminished on this side, giving us the ability to perceive our recent lives and your lives from a perspective we were mostly not privy to during our time on Earth. In one way, this may make our communications feel less personal because there is less of our old personality filtering everything.

On the other hand, because we are primarily communicating from the soul, rather than from the personality, our messages are full of love. Not sticky, gooey love, but pure love. This is not because we are all so noble and evolved, but because the nature of the soul is love and we inhabit a completely loving reality.

We are keenly aware that the most challenging place to rise above petty personality issues, unforgiving emotions, and limiting beliefs is during a human life on Earth.

From our vantage point, we now know that the more you drop the small stuff and live your soul's truth on Earth, the more fulfilling your lives will be. In addition, your spiritual maturity helps us evolve in at least two ways.

We are all part of a vast energy field fed by many sources, including everyone's individual and collective thoughts and feelings. The more each living person approaches life through the lens of the heart, the higher the quality of energy flowing between our realities and even beyond into the Universe.

Second, family members unconsciously carry dysfunctional patterns from generation to generation. Anyone in the family chain who is aware enough to see a limiting generational pattern in themselves and then to apply themselves and dismantle it has the potential to clear the entire lineage of that interference...past, present, and future.

You are capable of removing the fog created by hurts and grudges and fears, to see things as clearly as we can on this side. The possibilities for improving life on Earth this way, one person at a time, are endlessly uplifting.

And then when you pass over, you will start where

we have not even gone as yet. You will enter higher mansions of consciousness, experience, and contribution, more than you can imagine right now.

We are eager to share with you perspectives about our lives and deaths and where we are now for many reasons. We, who are on what you call the other side, are very vital members of the human family. We are part of an ongoing partnership with all life. One contribution we can make is to help you release the fear of death by expanding your hearts and minds to what really occurs.

And, as loving representatives of the universal human family, we wish to pass on our experiences with the hope that you will advance further in your lives than we did in ours.

This is why we have suggested the name "Why Wait" for this book. So, let's get on with it.

With love,

Jonathan, serving as spokesperson in this communication for members of the human family no longer physically with you

Chapter 1

Transmissions from People
Who Died Young

BEARING WITNESS TO how young people grow, develop, and fulfill themselves creates part of the wonder and richness of life. When someone dies at an early age, they have been deprived of a future. We have been robbed of participating in their life, loves, challenges, and delights.

From our Earthbound perspective, this is all true and incredibly painful. The expression we often use when a young person dies is, "They were cut down in their prime," illustrating how the loss is more poignant and leaving us bereft. Often, we are left feeling that dying young is terribly unfair.

It is unjust and there is also a bigger picture. The Transmissions from these young people reveal many uplifting truths. They each concur that dying does not hurt. They are happy on the other side. They are excited to share what they are learning about their recent lives and what truly matters. They would like us to take pleasure in them and to honor them by applying some of what they have discovered to our lives.

Concurrent with the horrific loss, and after the initial pain subsides, there are always opportunities to grow in the aftermath of a tragedy. Whenever possible, turning heart-wrenching grief into heart-opening contribution is the high road to take. Often, surviving parents and siblings embark on more fulfilling personal and career directions in their lives. Sometimes family members dedicate themselves to finding a medical cure, assisting other grieving parents, or championing causes, which honor their child by helping other young people in the world.

At the very least, the shock of losing someone young can be a wake-up call for the living to reprioritize what matters most in life and to embody those values. Above all, there is the opportunity to live with the daily deep appreciation that the gifts of life and of time are very precious.

"I made the most of my life. Therefore,
my life did not seem brief to me."
—Chris

Isabel Introduces her Friend Chris, Who Almost Graduated

Chris was a classmate of mine from grades six through twelve. He was born with a congenital disease. He underwent more surgeries than is even fathomable for any person, much less a kid. He was not expected to live past the age of twelve; he miraculously made it to eighteen. He passed away just two months shy of our high school graduation. Chris was really hoping to make it to graduation, but alas, he did not.

He was such an important part of our class, and his absence at graduation seemed simply wrong. I was the Master of Ceremonies for my high school graduation, and I felt that having a Transmission from him and sharing some of his words would be the perfect way to include him in our graduation...and I did just that. The Transmission from him was right on the money and "so Chris." It was heartfelt, wise, funny, and spunky, all at the same time. I could envision him saying every single word.

Chris was so inspiring...he was a skinny, little guy with a huge heart, an amazing sense of humor and the ability to work any crowd. His resilience was admirable and gave me the perspective early on that it is important to look at the big picture and rise above the petty stuff. It also taught me about gratitude...knowing him made me grateful for my own health and that of my family members. He inspired me to value human life more than I ever had and reminded me to always live in the present moment. I think he made me tougher, too. I recognized that a sports injury or the flu was nothing compared to the pain he was enduring every single day. He also showed me and all of our peers that the way you react to pain, illness, bad news, etc., is up to you and that you have the choice and ability to have a good attitude, keep your sense of humor, and be kind and caring to others despite any hardship.

These life lessons have impacted me in my now adult life. I am so grateful to Chris for having been a part of my life as a kid. I imagine that his short life and his little body were an inspiration to so many kids and adults alike. He demonstrated that the soul is so powerful and that the body is just a soul's "vehicle."

Although we never, ever wanted to lose Chris, I truly believe that he served his purpose in his life, and his life was complete. The fact that he departed this Earth just prior to our high school graduation was a blessing in disguise for the entire school. His passing served as a reality check for our senior class. It had the effect of making the somewhat out-of-control students take a step back and recognize that life is precious and fragile.

I would hazard a guess that this change in perspective may well have prevented drunk driving and other reckless behaviors, which in turn, likely saved a life or two as we all "sobered up" after his death and started taking better care of each other and ourselves.

I am forever grateful to Chris for all that he shared, accomplished, and taught us in his short life. I hope that he does reincarnate as the child of one of my classmates and that the world gets to experience his incredible soul once again. And, I am sure he will be certain to incarnate next in a very big, buff, tall, healthy body. He'll probably be a pro athlete in his next go-around!

—Isabelle Adams

To all my friends at graduation,

You know that one of the few things I wanted in my life was to graduate from high school with you. I know it was not a likely possibility, but it was a good goal, the kind that is just enough to be a stretch…a faraway goal, but intriguing and hopefully possible.

The only thing I want to tell you guys is that if you live each day one at a time and do everything you can each day without thinking about either the past or the future, even one day can seem like a very long and special time. A lot of people are feeling pity for me for not living very long, but I made the most of it. Therefore, my life did not seem brief to me.

But I was a vertically challenged dude, and that was a bummer for me! You know where I am; I can be tall and buff just by thinking of myself that way. If I hold that thought regularly, I stay that way. This is very cool.

Listen, if you guys hold the thought consistently of what you want to accomplish with your lives, your thoughts for the future will get programmed into you, and you will do it.

But don't get too serious about your futures, just put it all into now. I am seriously considering getting back into the born on the Earth scene again. I figure it won't be too hard to pick up where I left off…hmmm, maybe my soul will show up as one of your future kids!

But I do need some healthier genes next time around! That was just a joke. My mother will always be my favorite person. She loves me 100%, and I learned the most important thing ever from her. I learned that being lovable has nothing to do with how tall you are or how healthy you are or anything superficial. I know my mother also never expected she could love so much. Tell her that there is even more love available to share around. There is no beginning and no end limit to love.

So now, keeping with my recent reputation, I can't stay serious too long. I am happy here. I am healthy and tall and buff. I send you all little thought balls of appreciation. You know, like paint balls...let them burst all over you!

Chris

*"You would even agree that everyone has a time to go.
Why would I, or any young person, be the exception?"*
　　　　　　　　　　　　　–Sarah

Sarah Fell Overboard

Eight-year-old Sarah was on a sailing vacation with her family when suddenly, a storm came up. The winds howled, and the ocean became rough with waves as high as tall buildings. The wild rolling of the boat knocked her overboard. Given the weather conditions, it was impossible to rescue her. Sarah does not experience her death as a tragedy; she even cajoles her mother for reacting in that way.

> *Dear Mom,*
>
> *I want you to know that it did not hurt to die. There wasn't even time to be scared. If I had survived, I might have remembered what happened with a lot of fear, especially after hearing everyone's story about what happened…and I am sure that if I survived, I would also have a ton of injuries and pain to deal with, too… but moving so fast from life to death with no time in between was like flying peacefully in a dream. Don't be mad if I tell you it was sort of a fun feeling. I am really okay You are the ones making it into a horror story.*
>
> *The not-fun part is that I am here and you are there. I experience that we are still connected and always communicating no matter what. I wish you would see it that way, too. I can see you and hear you anytime I think of you or when you think of me. That's how I have heard from you how awful it was and continues to be.*

You see it all gloomy and that it was your fault. I see it as you love me, and I am living in a state of love where I am. Being here, where the world is about love, makes me happy. A world, which is all torn up, where people are mean and hurt each other and animals, does not make me happy. I would have felt that life is harsh in the world even if I lived to be 100 years old! You gave me love and shelter from most of the world storm, but there is no storm here, only where you are living.

You believe that you let me down and that makes you feel guilty, feeling like you are no better than all the other irresponsible people in the world. That is not true. You are my mother, and you gave me and taught me everything, and then it was time for me to go. You would even agree that everyone has a time to go. Why would I, or any young person, be the exception? Being old does not mean anything here. It seems to mean everything where you are.

I am helping so many children who pass over every day to feel at home and welcomed and happy. I am part of the welcoming committee. They call me the flower girl. I don't really get it, but you know I do love flowers.

Please see the big picture now. Two things are true at the same time: I am sad to not be with you in our life adventures every day; I am also fine where I am. Maybe the message for you is to be happy without any conditions or requirements for happiness.

I love you very much, Sarah

*"Buy flowers every week when you do the food shopping.
Think of them as if they are from me."*
−Ben Leavitt

_____Ben Leavitt Accidentally Overdosed

Ben was a recent inner-city high school graduate, seduced into the murky world of drugs and fast money who accidentally overdosed one night. The letter is to his mother. There is clear insight into the inner world of any addict, plus sage, loving advice to her.

Dear Mom,

Easy money, adrenaline rushes, danger, secret meetings...this might sound like espionage work. Add the drugs, alcohol, beating the law, underground connections and it sounds more like the Mafia. I was not part of either, but I was part of what you could call a small brotherhood dealing in and making drugs for sale on a small scale. It made us feel important.

I got into it like a game, a power game. Then the game became a habit; then the habit ran the game. Then the game had an ante, which grew and grew. Then one day, the stakes were life and death.

I did not mean to overdose; I was not trying to kill myself. I was in a game, which had no exit. I was addicted to the whole scene. That sent me to the next dare, to the next drug, to the next fix, and eventually, to the false move. When the moves are too hard to figure out, the game is over...and you are dead.

What I am doing right now is slowly peeling away layer upon layer of gooey, smoky, film-like stuff, which are layers of addiction. If this were on Earth, I would be in enormous pain and also irritable, angry, and aggravated going through withdrawal…but this is gentler and less painful. Slowly I am getting back to myself. It feels good.

What do I mean by smoky, film-like layers? Addicts construct frameworks of denial, rationalization, and lies. Think of each of these as a smoky film. As each one of these lifts, there is a pure glimpse of the real me that peeks through.

Addicts live in the heart of fear, and when you are there, no amount of reason, logic, help, or love can penetrate. NOTHING penetrates; it is only fear and survival. Now I am starting to feel again…like, who I was before the lies and the rest of the game I already told you about. I am getting un-numb. I am very excited about this.

The big thing for you is to not take my mistakes personally. I was an adult. You did great in raising me. There is no blame and no shame. Your son was a drug addict, and he was also a good person, a good friend, and sometimes even very funny. It's complicated and not all black and white. I did my best in the decisions I made, even if they were bad ones. The bad news is that I didn't have to die young. The good news is that I am out of the addiction game.

I am getting free of it all and learning so much. For the first time in forever, I am feeling relaxed. I am not chasing any more highs, and I am feeling no fear. There is no fear here.

I know you're driving yourself crazy with wondering why I got into the mess in the first place. I don't know *all the reasons yet; I will eventually. The main reason was boredom and the challenge of an interesting game. I should have gotten a job in espionage or something useful with an edge. That'll have to wait for my next life! What I can promise myself is that I will never again be an addict, thanks to the help I have now.*

I want to say a few more things about boredom: There are lots of kids like me who are bored in school. Only a few special teachers have any idea of who the kids really are, what makes them tick and how to challenge and coach them. Why? Because many of the teachers are sleeping in their own lives, which makes what they have to offer in school irrelevant. The kids who get in trouble are not lacking in smarts; they are lacking in finding any meaning in school. The solution is relevant learning offered by teachers who live meaningful lives themselves. Anyway, this subject still gets me upset. I didn't think I could still get stomachaches, but I guess I can.

Here is the absolute most important thing I have to share. I need you to know that I love you. I can see you clearly now. You are an angel. You are a gentle person. You like and need beauty and harmony. I get it that the horrors that go on in the world are almost more than you can bear. I am so sorry that my death has added to your burden. Please, please continue to focus on the beauty, which can be found in all things. There is even beauty in my passing. The exit I took has given me peace and healing. If this is what it took for me to get myself back, so be it.

My advice to you is to keep only the friends who are like you…gentle and loving. Enjoy flowers. I know you love flowers. Buy flowers every week when you do the food shopping. Think of them as if they are from me. I realize I am not buying them, but I am recognizing that you and beautiful flowers go together. Pay attention to your life now. Make it what you want. Keep it simple. Get rid of any riffraff. You know who I am talking about.

I will be in touch from time to time. For now, my feelings for you will be in flowers...wild flowers, too.

Your son, Ben

"It is a misperception to think adding another person, another possession, or another job is the missing element to happiness."

−Eliza

Tory Introduces Her Sister, Eliza, Who Only Lived Three Days

My earliest conscious memory of my sister is of my mom asking me to sit a few steps up on our stairs so she could tie my shoes. She was very pregnant and couldn't lean over. As an active two-and-a-half-year-old, I remember thinking this was very funny. That was forty-six years ago.

A few weeks after the shoe-tying memory, I remember being in the car with my dad on a rainy, dark night when he pulled over, started to cry and told me that my little sister, Eliza, who had been born two days earlier, had died due to many complications.

From that day on, my sister's early death became a buried and unhealed wound in our family. The pain was pushed under the rug, never to be dealt with in the light of day. I was an only child, and another child was never born.

Fast forward many decades, it occurred to me that it would be a great opportunity to ask Carol for a Transmission from my sister's soul. Over the years, Carol had already done very wonderful Soul Readings for me and for my children, and I thought perhaps a message from my sister might have some helpful insight and words of wisdom for me. Maybe it would help heal my own long-standing sadness surrounding her death...and I was also curious to learn more about the purpose of her short life.

When I read the Transmission from my long-ago lost, but never forgotten sister, I winced and then tears fell. Right away, Eliza clearly articulated the unspoken dynamics surrounding her conception and birth. This had to do with my parents, and of course, I would not have known this as a two-and-a-half-year-old. As an adult, I recognize all she describes about my parents. That part can still sadden me.

The takeaway from the Transmission for me is profound. This is a call to action for me to let go of family behavior patterns I no longer want to perpetuate in myself or to inadvertently pass on to my children. Eliza says clearly that she is learning that happiness is an inside job. I recognize this lesson is also true for me, and is actually a common theme in my family.

The most glaring example of the theme is that my dad long ago succumbed to the suicide of alcohol, feeling that he couldn't make things right for my mother —never learning that no matter how hard he tried to help, only she could resolve her unhappiness.

I can always wonder what it would have been like to have a sister. I can also see that holding onto the idea that "if only I had a sister…" is the old pattern of thinking my happiness is dependent on something or someone outside of myself. This is a huge insight.

So, I smile to myself, recognizing that from beyond the grave, my own sister is the most recent in a series of wise and helpful people in my life who have offered me the same three messages: We each must source our own peace and happiness from within; being vulnerable and open is healthy; and feeling pain, rather than pushing through and burying it, is the key to growing and then moving forward to live more fully. I am working on all three for myself.

Eliza's letter is a wonderful treasure, a reminder of the truths I need to practice and carry with me. I intend

her letter to be the catalyst to help me always remember to look inward for the peace and joy I strive for.
    –Tory Sultz

Dear Tory,

So here is a most interesting question: Why does a soul come in for such a short amount of time, and what purpose does that serve for all involved?

First of all, the incoming soul…mine in this case… knows ahead of time that this will not be a long stay in a viable body, so there are no unmet expectations, and there is no suffering. My soul agreed to come in ever so briefly to set an "experience stage" for the individuals in the family. My soul also had its learning opportunity, which I will tell you about later in this letter. A short presence and a quick exit trigger both emotional reactions and emotional opportunities for each person. The intention is growth, not self-punishment.

A grieving heart is always a cracked-open heart. For that moment, carefully constructed survival mechanisms and limiting unconscious patterns of thought and behavior are blown open. The stage is set for a life-altering positive breakthrough…or not.

It is a chance for each family member to redirect some aspect of their life for the better, if they choose.

It may be a hard thing to grasp, but when someone dies, each person is grieving something different, even though the trigger is the same. Your mother hoped another child would add to the amount of love in her life from children, give you a sibling, and perhaps most important, evoke more love from and closeness to her husband.

Your father was hoping that another child would make your mother happier and busier. This was not mean on his part. It was recognition of his personal shortcomings and the fact that he was busy with his career. He wanted her to be happy. Fathering children was important to him because it put him in touch with the miracle of life.

For you, the loss was that you could have had a sister to play with, also to pick on, but mostly my presence would have given you someone near your age at home; you had no comrade. A child's mind might have thought it was your fault, which absolutely was not the case. Of course no one knows how my presence would actually have played out.

I cannot tell you how I might have turned out: what kind of person or sister I would have been; whether or not we would have liked each other; how our parents would have taken to me; or any of those personality-related details. It was never part of the plan that I express myself in that way. I had no time to develop a persona…that was part of the deal. I got a free and quick trip to Earth with no strings.

What did I get out of it all? Your parents gave me the chance to objectively watch how adults project their hopes for solutions to their own stuff onto something or someone external. I also experienced compassion for why this is so. People want to feel loved and happy, as well they should. I needed to see that happiness is not about anything outside oneself. It is a misperception to think adding another person, another possession, or another job is the missing element to happiness.

I had been someone in other lives who dreamed a lot about how this or that would have made me so much more happy. I always had great expectations, and therefore, great disappointments. I didn't know to look inside myself, and if I had, I would not have known what to do.

My brief life was my opportunity to see my old misperception about happiness clearly and to learn. It set the stage for me to get on with being able to see myself as the source of my happiness in future lives. I have incarnated again and am still working on this!

Your sister, Eliza

> *"No one in their right mind would want the flow*
> *of love in your life to stop because I died."*
> —Michael

____Michael's Love Letter to His Fiancée

Michael was engaged to be married and looking forward to a long life when he was diagnosed with a terminal illness. This incredibly thoughtful letter is to his girlfriend, who stayed with him until he passed away. His words about the expansiveness of love and the potential of the human heart to evolve the world are an inspiration.

Dear Sweetheart,

First things first: I love you.

The entire time I was sick and dying I could not get rid of the idea that something must be the matter with me as a person. I figured I must be unworthy and unlovable to be so young, in love, and terminally ill. Either I was defective or God was enjoying a cruel joke at my expense. This obsessive, negative thinking gave me stomachaches, which I did not need. I had enough going on.

The self-doubt and inner turmoil got me really mad. Being mad gave me the fuel to fight my illness for a long time...but it turns out that mad does not help self-doubt at all. Being angry works like adrenaline, it was a temporary source of energy, which ultimately left me more exhausted. Like an addiction, I had to fire up the anger to higher levels of rage each time to get the so-called benefits. To do that, I would get into hating how I was wasting away and getting so skinny and ugly.

This explanation comes with a huge apology to

you for the many times that my anger spilled over to you. I am so sorry that I was often critical of you and not thoughtful enough of you. I learned big-time that when feeling awful physically and emotionally, it was near impossible for me to be considerate and loving of anyone. Yuk.

You get a Purple Heart for loving me in such difficult circumstances. You loved me even knowing we'd never be the couple who gets married and spends our lives together...and I know that being around me kicked up your own stuff, too. I continue to see you struggling to make sense of life, of us, and of your own life. I hope the rest of what I have to say to you can help you.

More than anything, I want to assure you that you are loved, all the time. You are loved, not just by me, but also by life itself, and so many people who love you, even people on this side whom you do not know! See if you can find a way to feel this in your heart, so you never doubt it. I can tell you that I can now see that love is the only thing that actually lasts. Love travels from one heart to another, as it also moves forever in and out of the Heart of all Creation.

Don't think I have gone religious on you. This has nothing to do with being religious. I can share this with you because I have been shown here how love circulates without end. Where I am, there is only love. That's also because our egos are mostly gone. It is so wonderful and easy, and there are no more inner battles.

Souls are about love, and love is everywhere here. I think if human beings could let go of their egos, love would be unmistakably everywhere on Earth, too. You remember how much I used to love the stars, right? So keep in mind that the stars are always shining even when the light of day makes it impossible to see them. The same is true with love from the soul...it is there all the time, but the ego makes it so hard to see and to feel with much certainty.

Here are some more important things I want you to know. I love you always, not just in the human sense, but in the eternal sense I have just tried to explain. And I am so relieved and relaxed. I can see that life is good, and there is a higher plan. This was the missing piece and the missing peace in my recent life. I feel so good now.

Real security comes from knowing in every cell of your being that you are love, and you are loved. With that foundation you can play and learn and experiment, sometimes get hurt and love with abandon. Make love your fuel.

Please go and live your life. You do me proud to move on. I am always in your heart, and you are in mine. The capacity of the heart is infinite, so there is always more room for loving more people in your life.

Know that when you find someone to marry, I will feel great. No one in their right mind would want the flow of love in your life to stop because I died. That would defeat the purpose of life, which I now know is to give and receive love in all its forms.

So, my dear, your boy has clearly "seen the light"!
Michael

"The most important thing I am learning at the
moment is that thoughts are so powerful."
　　　　　　　　　—Josh

__Josh Expands His World

Like most of us when we were kids, Josh never even
imagined he could get really sick and die in his teens.
Sadly, that is what happened. Among the insights in
this Transmission, Josh has discovered that our thoughts
and words contribute to what happens in our lives.

Dear Family,

Who would o'thunk that I would be the first of us
to chart this afterlife course? Truth is, I am fine. I can
see all of you if I focus my attention your way. I am with
new and old friends, and it is very interesting to not be
subjected to the laws of gravity. That is such a perfect
word, "gravity." It makes everything weigh a lot more
than necessary, and gravity also brings down people's
spirits.

Being a kid was fun because kids don't take things
too seriously. I mean, from a kid's-eye view, can you see
any benefits to becoming an adult? Adults all seem so
burdened and serious. True confessions: I could never see
myself growing old and being one of those heavy adults.

What I did not know until now was how powerful
those secret inner thoughts are. They are in there, but
they are being broadcast, and they can come true. Please
officer, "It was only a thought."

The most important thing I am learning at the mo-
ment is that thoughts are so powerful. They mobilize to

make things happen.

Where I am right now, every single thought plays out instantly in 3-D.

I can overwhelm myself by my own "junk mail" thinking, or I can truly enjoy clear, directed and positive thinking. If I think, "I am at the park," then boom, there I am at the park. If I think a scary thought, then I am right there, too. This is how it works here: Because every thought and wish plays out immediately, I have to pay super-close attention. For example, it makes me aware that most of my twisted sense of humor has to go...but I am using it a bit right now so you can recognize me.

Back to the point, this is a learning phase for me. First, this is about knowing what I want, then realizing that my thoughts coalesce into action...(aka) reality. For you, those thoughts and intentions take a lot longer to come to pass due to gravity...but I assure you they do come to pass. Here the process is instantaneous.

I am here to attest to the fact that dying is an illusion. I am just as alive as you are...perhaps even more so, because nothing here is about fear. So there is no impending sense of failure or judgment or pressure. Nothing is hidden from self or from anyone else. The idea is to see what your thoughts create, where they take you, and to see if this is what you really want. I get it that this is also how thoughts work where you are. Note: This is a very worthwhile thing to at least think about.

I am also into music here. This is so amazing: I can look at a tree and hear its song, and then sing it or play it. I can feel the tree's appreciation of being recognized. The love in all this blows me away! A tree is only one example of this experience…the phenomenon applies to any living thing. Oh, and even to some things I used to not realize were living…like rocks, stars, and planets. Actually, everything seems to be alive.

My world is so expanded; I cannot tell you how excited I am. I knew there had to be more to life than what I was able to experience.

Now to heavier things: shift background music to somber. First, I am truly sorry for the pain I have caused you. Everyone should wake up to how much they are loved while they are alive. That awareness would be so helpful, "Oh, you mean you love me even though…?" What kind of newfound freedom and acceptance is that? I never realized that so many people loved me. I know that now, and I can feel it where I am. Please know that this knowledge is not too late. It is very useful right now because getting it accelerates my progress here.

This reminds me of something I want to mention to you. When you have thoughts or conversations out loud wondering what you might have, could have, should have said or done in relation to me…you are beating up on yourselves, and I can feel this. Just so you know, it feels lousy. From where I sit, everyone has multiple choices of where and when to exit the highway of life. One of my exits came up suddenly, and here I am.

The best you can do is to forget about blame altogether, and live the way you want to be happy and have meaning right now. Learn from me that thoughts have an effect on the thinker and on the thinkee. Pay more attention to what you say and think if you consider this useful. (I hope you do.)

I am off to play some sports. This is another thing. Imagine this: You already know that where I am, what you think…happens. In sports you have to focus precisely, or it is complete chaos. I like this practice of very on-purpose thoughts, which translate into great athleticism. Everything I am telling you is science fact where I am and applies to Earth life, too.

I love you all. If some of you are curious to interact with me, just be still and call me in. You will feel my presence. Some of you have already experienced me with you. When I am there, you get a particular sensation in your body. Trust it.

Your son and brother, Josh

P.S. You ask if there is anything you can do for me. After you keep what you want, see if any of my friends want anything I used to own and give it to them. I have you all in my heart, and you have me in yours, which is really the point. Also, when you can, please be happy for me, and go for it right now where you are.

"The first thing I have realized about this thing of living and dying is that you never realize how many people are affected by your life and by your death."

−Mark

Mark Makes a Surprising Discovery

Mark was an accomplished athlete who loved to push the envelope and take risks in his sport. He was a mountain climber, and on this fateful day in the high Sierras, the weather suddenly deteriorated and so did the conditions. He slipped and fell to his death. This letter is to his (then) girlfriend. His greatest surprise is to discover how much people he knew, and even strangers, cared about him. We are more important to each other than he ever realized.

Dear Nicole,

Okay, I am able to observe everything that is going on with people at home, including all the arrangements for my funeral. I am not alone. I am with other friends who are not alive in your world, and also with others who are taking care of me and helping me understand what has happened. They tell me I am sort of in shock, and that I am definitely alive here, just not in the same reality. All my senses are working; I don't even have a headache. I am trying to get a grip on all this, which is taking a lot of concentration.

The first thing I have learned about this thing of living and dying is that you never realize how many people are affected by your life and your death. I cannot believe how many people are talking about me and thinking about me, and wondering what happened to me. Then I also see how what happened to me brings up lots of emotions for them and reminds them of other things in their lives, having nothing directly to do with me. It is amazing for me to watch.

I never realized I was so important to so many people...even people I don't know and who didn't really know me. So, they can't even say, "Oh, he was a good kid or a bad kid," or anything about me, 'cause they didn't know me. Still, they are saddened, upset, and even confused. Wow, this might have been good to know sooner. How can people who don't even know you feel they love you? Obviously, something is going on that I am just beginning to understand.

So, since I do not know a lot yet, the thing I can say with assurance is this: I can see right now how many of you are feeling guilty thinking things like, "What did I do wrong, or where did I fail when it came to him?" I can tell you that guilt is useless; it does not improve anything. In a way, it is like a pity party, unless you take action.

If you see something in your life or in yourself that you would like to make better, do it right now and keep the change you make from now on. You will not only be happier yourself, but improving yourself will have an invisible, positive effect on so many other people. Sounds dumb, but I can see from here how everyone is more connected than I knew or imagined. It is sort of awesome.

Please tell all of my friends and my parents that I am still around and mostly fine. I am not afraid, and I definitely did not realize that what I was doing could lead to my death. You can probably feel me around you at times…or when you think of me and then notice it suddenly gets windy, that is me saying "hello."

I am sorry I never knew so many things…including that I didn't say I love you to you or to other people. I do love all of you.

Later, Mark

"When you die, the fear is over."
—Pete

___Pete Died in Combat

This is a Transmission from Pete, who died after being wounded in a battle overseas. It is written to one of his close Army buddies. This is a poignant description of how he was met by fellow soldiers on the other side. He also reminds us to call upon loved ones no longer alive when we need support.

Dear Bud,

When you die, all the fear is over. Like you are in one bad movie about adrenaline and heat, stench and war, and then that movie ends, and you step into the daylight. I was met by groups of men who have already died, and I recognized a few of them.

They greeted me like a brother who has come home into the arms of the best family you could ever imagine. I said something dumb to them like, "I thought all of you are supposed to be dead." And they answered right back, "We are." Then there was a lot of laughing together, 'cause you get it, you are dead, too. And yet everyone is fine and whole and content. We are just having a matter-of-fact conversation about what happened to me. No one is wounded here. No one is sick or deformed. We all have a sense of humor. The feeling is being in the best brotherhood thing you could ever imagine.

At more or less the same time, other loyal men of the brotherhood escorted my no-longer-functioning physical body to my parents' home. It was very tough for them.

They were half expecting this to have happened to me, but when it happens, that's another story.

    Everyone, please know that I am fine so you can go on with your lives. I want you to be happy and enjoy all that you have. This is how to honor me.

    Pete

P.S. I try to show up for you all when you need a hand or a buddy to lean on for a minute. That's what buddies do. My presence is invisible to you, but maybe the hairs on your arms stand up a bit when you think of me, and then you'll know that I am there.

Pearls of Wisdom

Souls are ageless, and soulful knowledge and wisdom shine through these Transmissions. A common thread of awareness in these pages is that we are all interconnected more than we realize in life and even after death.

The energy we contribute to the matrix of life via our emotions, states of being, and actions affects everyone, including the souls who have passed. They assure us they are happy and fine where they are. They say the best way to honor them and to positively contribute to them is for us to be happy and to live well. Here are some of their suggestions for experiencing more happiness.

"…If you live each day one at a time and do everything you can each day without thinking about either the past or the future,

even one day can seem like a very long and special time." –Chris

"Maybe the message for you is to be happy without any conditions or requirements for happiness." –Sarah

"Please, please continue to focus on the beauty, which can be found in all things. There is even beauty in my passing. The exit I took has given me peace and healing." –Ben

"...Happiness is not about anything outside oneself. It is a misperception to think adding another person or another possession or another job is the missing element to happiness." –Eliza

"Make love your fuel. I think if human beings could let go of their egos, love would be unmistakably everywhere on Earth, too." –Michael

"Thoughts are so powerful...they coalesce into action...the idea is to see what your thoughts create, where they take you and to see if this is what you really want." –Josh

"If you see something in your life or in yourself you'd like to make better, do it right now and keep the change you make from now on. You will not only be happier yourself, but improving yourself will have an invisible, positive effect on so many other people... everyone is more connected than I knew or imagined." –Mark

"Everyone, please know that I am fine so you can go on with your lives. I want you to be happy and enjoy all that you have. This is how to honor me." –Pete

___Why Wait Meditation:
Making Gratitude your Attitude

Being happy from the inside-out brings inner peace even when the external circumstances in life are challenging. The key to experiencing inner happiness is living life through the lens of an open heart. When the heart is open, it connects us to the higher intelligence and unconditional love in the soul, and the soul connects us to Source. When that powerful heart/soul link up is active, the biochemistry of well-being is released into our bodies. In that state, you can be mad or sad or glad and simultaneously experience inner peace.

The big question is how to do this in the midst of all the rock and roll of daily life and all the commercial messages promising us we'll be happy if only we buy this or that. External fixes are only temporary. Real happiness is an inside job.

The answer is to practice gratitude. It is scientifically proven that feelings of gratitude open the heart. Gratitude rearranges our focus to the "glass-half-full" perspective on life, which is not just a cliché. When your attitude toward life is gratitude, the results include: an open heart, a robust immune system, more joy, and more inner peace, regardless of what life brings.

Here is a simple practice to use every day. It works, and the benefits are cumulative.

○ *Gently close your eyes, and take a few deep, relaxing breaths.*

○ *Now bring to your awareness five things large or small for which you are grateful today. It can be simply that you are grateful you are breathing or that the sun is shining or your dog is lying near you right now.*

○ *Take the time with each item to register the feeling of gratitude in your body.*

○ *Feeling gratitude in the body is what creates the magic.*

○ *Now allow yourself to feel gratitude for your life and for all of life.*

○ *Open your eyes and smile.*

○ *Repeat this as many times a day as you like. Over time, this will change your life and up your happiness quota.*

Chapter 2

Transmissions from People Who Took Their Own Lives

ONE OF THE MOST DISTURBING and shocking experiences is when someone commits suicide. What happens to people who take their lives is a controversial topic, which has been addressed in different ways by mystics, philosophers, religious teachings, and indigenous traditions. The conclusions cover the gamut from suicide is a sin requiring divine punishment to taking one's life is an act of desperation deserving of compassion and forgiveness.

Over the years, I have worked with clients who have lost someone to suicide. As you can imagine, they sought two significant pieces of information: What motivated the loved one to take their own life? And, what negative consequences might occur for doing this?

In these Transmissions, three important concepts are repeatedly shared. First, there is a universal awareness that taking one's life is the last option. Second, though taking one's life is the ultimate act of free will, it is used only in situations of utter despair. Third, there is no damning punishment. However, the patterns of thinking, acting, and believing that led to such hope-lessness and dire action require healing, both in the afterlife and in subsequent incarnations. Resolving these deep-seated issues requires willingness, commit-ment, and perseverance.

And finally, no matter what circumstances may have precipitated these people to commit suicide, no matter how old or young they were when they took their lives, all of these Transmissions include sincere ex-pressions of love for those they left behind.

> *"I wanted to make sure no one I knew would think I killed myself because of them."*
>
> —Tom

___Mary Introduces Her Son Tom, Who Explains His Choice

The loss of a child through suicide is a death that brings a grief so powerful that, as a mother who was caught unprepared for my son Tom's death, I did not know what to grab onto to keep myself from perishing also. My son Tom and I were close. People who knew us often commented how much we were alike. We loved life and had the desire to seek new adventures where others may not have been bold enough to tread.

Tom was thoughtful, intelligent, and very affectionate; he made sure that every member of our large family knew he loved them. As only one example, I cherish a letter Tom wrote to his older brother who had been called to active Army duty during the Bosnian crisis in 1999. "These are scary days here at home," Tom wrote. "We think of you daily, hourly, or at times, more often. The television is often on CNN Headline News...it gives us a sense of closeness with you and the other soldiers over there. I would trade places with you in a minute. This family loves you very much. You are such an important part of my life... such a good brother...such a good person."

Tom's death was a moment of great need for me. Carol Mann was the first professional person I contacted immediately after I learned of Tom's death. Her Transmission from him was "so Tom." Every word of that Transmission was like a neon sign flashing light, love, and understanding from Tom to me. He knew I would be struggling with his loss, as indeed I was.

As I have already mentioned, love was a theme in Tom's world, though Carol did not know this about him. And the love Tom expressed in the Transmission affected me profoundly. I could feel that the bond of love we shared was not broken even in death.

He loved nature, and before he took his own life outdoors that fateful winter, he wrote with his footprints in the snow, "I Love You All." I noticed right away how he shared in the Transmission that he wanted every family member and close friends to know how much he loved each one.

No words can describe the shock and pain of that loss, and no words can truly describe the comfort and road to recovery that the Transmission through Carol Mann has given me.

    —Mary Rodgers

Dear Mom,

I am fine, and for me right now, that means I am out of pain, which is the biggest relief. For me, the pain of not being able to be myself or feel like myself or move forward in life like myself just became intolerable. It was like living a shadow of myself...like someone who is paralyzed and can think about the idea of walking, but cannot move their body.

I was feeling like a mental paraplegic. I could think about how I wanted a medical career and marriage and a family, but I could not act on any of it. Somewhere along the line I was also on the way to ulcers, and God knows what else was physically wrong with me from my intense distress.

When an animal feels trapped, their terror is total,

and they do whatever survival things they can to get free. They even hurt themselves or kill themselves in the effort. I felt trapped just like a desperate animal, and the only way out for me was to leave the world and my suffering. It sounds crazy, but knowing that taking my life was an option became a freedom, which gave me peace for the first time in years.

The choice to commit suicide does not have to be exercised, I know that, and I tried for years to not pull the trigger. I made bargains with myself to try this or that medication and therapy for a certain amount of time to see if I could feel better. Nothing seemed to work, so I began to plan. Strategizing my end made me feel better...it gave me some sense of control and hope for relief. Though you experienced my death as a sudden horrific discovery, I had thought out this course of action for a long time, way before doing it.

I considered my plan an act of love toward myself... that I love myself enough to know when it is time to check out and start over.

In my own way and as part of my preparation, I made it a point to tell people I love how much they meant to me. I wanted you and everyone in the family, plus my friends, to hear from me that I loved all of you. I did this on purpose, person by person, because I wanted to make sure no one would think I killed myself because of them.

I also thought a lot about the most honorable way to do this. That's why I went into the woods, a place you know I loved. It was just my time to return to the Earth. I felt really peaceful and spiritual about doing this. I also felt close to nature, to you all, and to God.

I am so very sorry for causing you to suffer. I hope you can someday understand that this was about me getting myself out of my pain. This is not about what any one of you in the family could have done or should have done or might have done. This is not about you.

I have already learned so much. You know that I wanted to be in a healing profession. I now have so much compassion for people who are in chronic pain of any sort. Long-term pain can block out everything else a person knows and stands for. I know this now from my firsthand experience. I am learning compassion for myself, too.

I am welcomed where I am. You might say I am in a situation of "intensive care," where love washes over me and through me every moment. It probably sounds odd to you, but I am even breathing love in and out. Rather than pure oxygen for resuscitation, I am breathing pure love. There is no judgment toward me, and by now, almost none left from within me, either.

For now and forever, I love you. That never changes. Please allow yourself to feel this from me so that you know it is real. I come to you often, and I know you talk to me. I hear you. I am hoping that my love and all I have told you can bring you a sense of peace.

Your son, Tom

*"I apologize for giving you the example that
the way to live your life is to hide everything
inside and never to ask for help."*

–Joseph Holtzer

Joseph Apologizes and Explains

Joseph Holtzer was an attorney with a long and successful career, whose suicide was totally unexpected by his
family. His death was equally shocking to colleagues
and clients. This letter to his daughter, Holly, reveals the
inner demons, which led to the decision to end his life.

Dear Holly,

Where to start: With an apology and an explanation.

*I am now on what you call "the other side," where
there are no consequences for saying what I need to say,
and yet I still have a sense of trepidation communicating with you now. I am concerned about your reaction.
(Sigh) That shows me, I still have a lot of work to do on
expressing my truth, regardless of how I imagine others
will take it.*

*This was the crux of my hidden pain all my life.
Every decision I made whether the outcome was considered "good" or "bad" was based on fulfilling someone
else's expectations...someone else's idea of what I ought
to do or say or be. I don't mean that I was a goody-goody;
I was very angry inside.*

*But, on the outside, I did things all my life to please
my parents, to please my friends, to please my partner,
to please my professional colleagues...to do the "right"
thing, to be the "perfect" person in all my many roles.*

What built up in me over the many years was an intense feeling of being trapped and then being suffocated by all the "shoulds," obligations, and responsibilities. I do not regret my work, my marriage, my family, my friends, or my profession, but I did a lot of "acting" in my many roles, and I now see that as a huge mistake.

Others may have seen me as a competent, easygoing, together guy because that is how I conducted myself...but inside, I was screaming. I was dying to just jump out of my skin; I was dying to let out my real self. By then, I did not even know what my "real" self meant or who I was.

It may seem incomprehensible, but as I got older and more successful, I felt more and more hopeless...that it was too late to break out. It was too late to build a new foundation and too late to live my life differently. I just felt like a living robot, getting more and more numb, more and more out of touch with myself.

I fell into a deep sense of loss and hopelessness... all on the inside, not telling anyone. I wish giving you a medical diagnosis and leaving it at that would say it all. At the time, I felt the last decision left for me was to take my life. I didn't even know if I had the courage to do that. I guess I did.

When I did the deed, I was shocked at what a mess I had made. I was looking down at my body, which was odd. But what a mess! And what emotions I stirred up in everyone in the family, and friends and colleagues. All my life I was afraid to make a mess, and there it was at last.

Sounds crazy, but I feel free. I know I have a lot to

work out, to understand, and to set straight. There is so much to unravel in order to rediscover who I am. Then, there is learning how to live my truth and not be so dependent on the validation of others.

The good news is that it is so peaceful and accepting here. No one imposes anything; no one needs or expects anything from me or from each other. Everyone is here as I am, to see the workings of our own self-created pressures.

The goal for everyone in my "class" is to discover who we are and what we are like being ourselves. This is wonderful for me. I know I have a very long way to go before I could practice all I am learning here in a new life in your Earth reality. I certainly aspire to learn how to be myself no matter what others think, and at the same time remain open to self-improvement.

I apologize for giving you the example that the way to live your life is to hide everything inside and never to ask for help. I apologize for not giving you or anyone any idea of my real demons. I did not share with you all because in my anger and suffocation, I did not want help. I was into suffering like a martyr, and I did not want to be dissuaded from my course of action.

Most of all, I apologize to you...who would have helped me if I had asked...I am sorry I made you feel helpless. You are brilliant and capable. It was never my intent to cause pain; it was my plan to end my own suffering.

I love you and admire you. Please, please, in your life, do not follow in my professional footsteps unless this is truly your calling.

Always and forever, you are my beloved daughter.

"For all the difficulty I have caused you, and for all the
love I have deprived you of, I ask your forgiveness."
—Phyllis Tucker

_____Maggie Tucker Introduces Her Mother, Phyllis, Who Confides in Her

My mother took her life when I was a little girl, too young to grasp that adults have their own inner demons, burdens, and shortcomings. When I first heard about the Transmissions, I was a bit skeptical but open to seeing what would come of it. I remember being surprised that I could hear my mom's voice through the words. It was a really heart-warming experience. After years of emptiness, suddenly here was a message of love from my mom. At the time I read it, I was sick and estranged from most of my family, and having lost my mom at a young age, I didn't have many things to remember her by. The Transmission felt like a new piece of her, something that I could hold on to and add to my memories of her. It brought her back into my life at a time when I was close to losing everything, including myself.

This communication encouraged me to try to connect with her on my own. I began talking to her and asking for signs that she was out there listening. I started finding crow feathers on my daily walks. This was significant because the sound of crows cawing is something I associate with the house I grew up in with her. To this day, my automatic reaction to seeing crows is to say, "Hi, mom," to them. I often see them unexpectedly and in strange places.

It was also painful and hard to read some of what she said. My mom was everything to me. It was sad to

hear her say that she gave up too easily, that she felt there wasn't enough to keep her here and that after her death, she realized our love for each other could have been enough. It could have been enough. She was a strong, tough woman on the outside, always helping others and changing people's lives for the better. I wish she could have done the same for herself.
 —Maggie Tucker

Dearest lovely daughter,

I have been looking forward to talking with you so much, and now that it is really happening, I am nervous. I am feeling overwhelmed by emotion, something I haven't experienced in a long time. There is no fear here, and feeling nervous is a form of fear, which I have just brought up in myself. I have been living in an environment, which is only about love. Fear certainly dominated my life.

Taking my life was about my fear of living. I did not feel there was enough love in my life. To me, the world was a cold, hostile place. One life experience after another seemed to prove this. I felt lost, inadequate, helpless, and incompetent. I became obsessed with self-pity. All I wanted was to find a way out. In my misery and depression I was totally convinced that you and everyone else would be better off without me. I considered that having me around was like having a disease in the room, which needed eradication.

I was blinded completely by the hole I dug for myself. I could not see that the answer to enough love in my life was right in front of me. All the time, the answer was you, and you were right there. I adored you. My love for you and yours for me, mother-daughter, would have been more than enough to bring joy to anyone's life...but, completely lost in my darkness, I could not see that then.

My sorrow is so profound as I realize my death deeply wounded you. It is no wonder you felt abandoned. I am ashamed for creating so much pain. For all the difficulty I have caused and for all the love I have inadvertently deprived you of, I ask your forgiveness.

I have done a lot of work on myself since my death. As I mentioned, where I am now, no one can delude themselves by thinking there is not enough love. I have learned how I gave into fear and self-doubt, which eventually killed me. Though time as you measure it does not exist on this side, I can say that in the many years since my death, I have forgiven myself as well.

The next step for every soul, once they have filled their unique learning requirements on this side, is preparation to incarnate again in the physical Earth reality. The nervousness I experienced earlier is a helpful reminder that when I do incarnate again, those human feelings will inevitably come up. I know I am capable of staying my higher course. What I will be working on in my next Earth lives is the ability to create love, share love and enjoy the abundant love available in so many ways in a physical life on Earth.

This leads me to my heartfelt appreciation of you and your incredible resiliency and inner strength. Themes related to trust are common to everyone in our family. What I admire about you most is that you have demonstrated the inner strength and courage to rebuild your trust in yourself, in others, and in life. You are shedding the limitation of fear, and I see you now creating the life you want and finding joy.

I honor you for facing the issues in your life, and working with them to heal yourself. You are my inspiration for what is possible.

Bless you. I love you and always have, and always will.

Your Mom

P.S. As to my ashes, I agree that it's time to scatter them. I trust you to choose a beautiful location where the winds blow free.

"In my life I was craving intensity because I mistakenly assumed intensity was equal to meaning."

–Aaron

____Aaron Finds Meaning

Aaron was a bright young man whose loving parents had the financial means to provide all their children with the comforts of an affluent lifestyle and the benefit of the best education. As you will read, even this privilege did not provide answers for Aaron as he struggled so desperately to find meaning in life. Aaron shares with his father how he mistakenly sought out intensity, thinking that was the same as finding meaning.

Dear Dad,

This is difficult. Please keep on reading because it gets better.

I know how much pain and suffering I have caused you, and what a disappointment I have been to you. It is tough to have to tell others that your son killed himself. I guess it can also be embarrassing, and then people offer sympathy, but their sympathy is all mixed up with pity and relief that it wasn't their son, and who knows what else.

What I could never cope with is all those kinds of things I just mentioned. Sum it up as superficial social behavior: people's lack of authenticity, the thousand ways people invent to never make real contact and the morass of self-serving agendas. There's more: endless pressures to be this or that or to say this or that, and hollow definitions of success and fulfillment. It all made for such clatter and noise in my head that it was impossible for me to ever ask myself what might make up my happiness on my own terms.

My story is not very interesting. It is about the typical person who is very sensitive, who on the surface has it pretty good…and who on the inside is going nuts from no way to connect and find meaning in this world. I found some people's contributions to my life kind and well intended, and I found most people are asleep. My story is about someone who could not find his way out of the bag… and the world got too suffocating. So, thinking about how to escape and get out of the pain became the quest.

Here is the interesting part, which I have come to find out after passing over. Now I can see graphically that how a person thinks determines how he perceives everything. It is like the old glass-half-full/half-empty idea. If you think the glass is half empty, then it is half-empty to you; that is your reality. It isn't necessarily true, but it is true for you. I see that people do this kind of thing all the time with everything in life. All along the glass is only a glass with an amount of water in it.

So I have been able to see how that got started for me. I got off to a few negative perceptions of people and the world, along with a bunch of fears and shaky self-esteem. Soon enough, no matter who was in front of me, I conditioned myself to see only their flaws.

Then when I got into substance abuse, it just made my negative worldview more pronounced, and my own brain chemistry being out of whack made it even worse. It got too hard to sort out the truth about anything. I never realized how powerful the mind is…or I should say how powerful my mind was in creating all that I experienced.

Now, killing myself was one lousy way to have discovered all this, but it worked. I am not the type to accept that the fire is hot unless I put my hand in it. I needed an intense experience to get me to a new level of awareness.

In my life I was craving intensity because I mistakenly assumed intensity was equal to meaning. What I was really missing was seeing life the way it is…people the way they are. That would have been intense enough and real. Just like that glass with a certain amount of water in it, life is just life until you add your own perception to it.

Where I am is like having an ever-present easel, a blank canvas, and a set of paints. I have the ability to create with my thoughts. Whatever I imagine shows up on the canvas. It is remarkable and so creative.

I never realized while I was alive that I was also creating with my thoughts. Unfortunately, at that time I was creating the negative painting of my life. Everyone's doing this with positive and negative thoughts and beliefs. OMG, and then we "paint" all over each other, too.

I am learning a new enthusiasm for creativity, for perception, for how meaning is created, and possibly even what life is about. Having this awareness gives me so much joy and inner peace. Now I am truly interested in things, rather than how I used to categorically dismiss everyone and everything. For me to see things for what they are and make my choices based on what's real is a huge discovery for me.

I need a lot more time before I have this down and can apply it to living on Earth again. Actually, I am still on the Earth, but in an alternate reality…one which is lighter than where you are, but is basically in the very same location.

Dad, I know you are a good man. Please laugh again and enjoy yourself more…smell the flowers…go outdoors…relax. You have the soul of a poet, and you don't share it. Please do from now on. What is heavy about life is placing the perception on life that things are so serious. If that is your lens, then everything in your life is a burden.

What if you let out the joy, the sensitivity, the ability to see poetry and beauty in simple things, which you have? Live like the old Beatles song "Imagine," which you always loved. Go for it!

I love you. I am not hung up on anything. I do not blame either of you for anything. This was not fun for anyone, and yet it is the way I have learned so much.

Lucky you, you can choose to benefit from my experience and from what I am sharing here. Use it, please, to grow while you are still alive. Then your experiences in this reality where I am will be even more enriched.

Be good to yourself…so easy to say and so hard to do, I know.

Love, Aaron

____*Pearls of Wisdom*

All the people in this chapter make it a point to reveal the inner conflicts and personal demons that convinced them to believe (whether true or not) that the only way to get out of their own pain was to take their lives. On the other side they are no longer suffering, and they are healing.

An important takeaway from their disclosures is that the decision to kill oneself is an act of personal desperation, not a choice lightly taken, and not about anyone else. This understanding invites us to open our hearts with compassion for their suffering, and compassion for our inability to change the outcome.

"The choice to commit suicide does not have to be exercised, I know that, and I tried for years to not pull the trigger. I made bargains with myself to try this or that medication or therapy for a certain amount of time to see if I could feel better. Nothing seemed to work, so I began to plan." –Tom

"It may seem incomprehensible, but as I got older and more successful, I felt more and more hopeless…I just felt like a living robot, getting more and more numb, and more and more out of touch with myself…It was never my intent to cause pain; it was my plan to end my own suffering." –Joseph

"To me the world was a cold, hostile place. One life experience after another seemed to prove this. I felt lost, inadequate, helpless, and incompetent. I became obsessed with self-pity. All I wanted was a way out." –Maggie

"My story is not very interesting. It is about the typical person who is very sensitive, who on the surface has it pretty good... and who on the inside is going nuts from no way to connect and find meaning in this world." –Aaron

___Why Wait Meditation: Practicing Compassion

This is a true story. Notice how your body responds as you continue reading it.

> A woman was rushing out of the supermarket with her arms full of groceries. Seemingly out of nowhere, a man crashed into her almost knocking the two of them over. The groceries she'd been carrying scattered all over the ground. The woman immediately lashed out at the man screaming, "What the hell's the matter with you, are you freaking blind or something?" Then she looked at him...gasped exclaiming, "Oh my God!"...as she saw that he was blind.

> In that instant realization of the truth, her fury evaporated, her heart opened, and she was flooded with feelings of compassion.

> The focus shifted immediately away from her initial response of being "wronged" and turned into the awareness that the blind man was doing the best he could. Bumping into her was not intentional. And she had sincere feelings of concern for him.

Compassion is not about pity, nor is it about condoning hurtful behavior. Compassion is seeing "what is" without judgment through the eyes of an open heart. The lens of the heart replaces survival reactions with caring responses.

Here is a meditation to experience the feeling of compassion.

○ *Find a comfortable and quiet place to sit, where you will not be interrupted for ten minutes.*

○ *Close your eyes and take three deep breaths.*

○ *Focus your awareness on your physical heart.*

○ *Imagine you can literally inhale and exhale through your own heart. Breathe through your heart.*

○ *As you do this, bring into your awareness someone you know and care about who is currently suffering.*

○ *As you hold them gently in your heart, silently extend to them your heartfelt wish that their suffering be eased.*

○ *Notice how this feels in your body.*

○ *Refocus your awareness on your heart.*

○ *Silently extend the same heartfelt wish to yourself, that any suffering you are currently experiencing also be eased.*

○ *Gently open your eyes.*

The more you practice compassion, the more it will become a state of mind, a feeling, and a way of being. With this view of life, you will discover a very freeing, universal truth: We are all doing the best we can with what we are given in any moment.

As consistently as possible, live with an open heart. When the heart is full, suffering has no space.

Chapter 3

Transmissions from Mothers to Their Children

SOME OF THE MOST enthusiastic messages from the other side are from mothers who are eager to share their experiences and personal insights with their living children. What they communicate illuminates what happens after death and offers all of us the opportunities for healing.

The first theme all these women communicate is that no matter how effectively or ineffectively they expressed love to their children during their lives, these soulful Transmissions reveal the universal truth of unconditional "mother" love.

Something else you will notice is how often in these Transmissions the women (and sometimes the men in other chapters) describe how happy they are to enjoy a whole, pain-free, and younger physical appearance. Clearly this is a relief after the many ways the physical body might have become debilitated or disfigured in death. Also, the ability to "select" some aspects of how one "looks" is an application of how thought immediately translates into reality on the other side.

It's interesting to note how thought, attention, and intention influence our total well-being in body, mind, and spirit. This is a hot topic in neuroscience research right now, and findings point to the fact that we can use our intention to change the architecture of our brains.

We also learn that it sometimes takes being on the other side, where the soul is in charge and the ego is dismantled, for people to see into themselves clearly. Many of these letters allow us to witness how these women were the products of their own inner limitations and the formative circumstances of their lives.

Hopefully, this insight opens your heart to greater compassion toward your own mother, whether or not she is alive. We are all given the chance to better our lives by letting go of old hurts in light of the awareness that everyone does the best they can with what they are given.

Happily, if there were ways our mothers were not, in our estimation, the best they could have been for us, the course correction is in our own hands. Here it is: We get to be the kind of parent we wish we had.

Whether or not you are a mother or a father, be aware that offering others a sense of deep support, nurturance, and caring is by definition making an uplifting contribution to their well-being.

"I experienced the miracle of each of you."
–Your Mom

____My own Mother – Only Love Remains

The last time I saw my mother, I brought her a calendar for the year 2005, which I had created using photos of her original oil paintings for the glossy cover photo and the images for each month. As she turned the pages, carefully taking in the art, she mused out loud, "These paintings are so beautiful."

"These are photos of some of your paintings, mom," I offered brightly.

"I really did these?" she replied, but she did not remember; the disease had stolen her memory.

"At least she still recognizes beauty," I thought to myself. "That's always been her joy."

My mother loved beauty and was captivated by the elegance of form, whether that was in nature, in art, or in her home. She loved cut flowers, collected art, cooked elegant food for her dinner parties, created artistic centerpieces and made me set the table correctly whether or not we had company.

I once commented to her that she put herself together each day like a perfectly composed still-life painting come to life. She was very pretty, and no matter how early in the morning, my mother always greeted me and my brothers groomed and dressed for the day.

She was the reason our family went on summer vacations to the country or to the ocean, where I spent a lot of time outdoors and learned the names of birds and wild flowers and seashells and some of the constellations in the night sky. I truly loved my childhood with the rich experiences and the love she and my father gave my brothers and me.

We also had plenty of struggles over the years. In my most rebellious and resentful moments I thought of her as the wicked queen in *Snow White* who did not want to allow me a place in the kingdom. She was very hard on herself and critical of others, which of course included me. Most of the time I was able to brush off whether or not she liked how I dressed or comments about some of my friends. However, I always wished she would acknowledge my passion for exploring worlds beyond the five senses. Though she was plenty intuitive, that did not fit into her worldview; and therefore, did not happen while she was alive.

My mother wanted her life to be many steps up from her parents' immigrant circumstances, and she had the will, the smarts, and determination to make that happen. She saw to it that she went to college, and she was the only girl in her family who did. She also went on to earn a graduate degree and pursued a professional career decades before the advent of "Women's Lib" and the "Women's Rights Movement."

She also married a great man. My father was very intelligent with a good heart and a great sense of humor; he adored her and supported her in all ways, as she was equally inspired toward him. She would always say he was her best friend and lover; he would say the same of her, and they meant it. They had a wonderful relationship and children who turned out to be good people. She truly created a fulfilling life.

With all that, she also wanted to be an accomplished artist. When my father died, he left her a letter to be opened after his death. In it, he encouraged her to go to art school and fulfill that part of her dream. With his eternal encouragement, my mother graduated from the Museum of Fine Arts School in Boston with a degree in oil painting. She was 80 years old at her graduation. Her specialty was what she called "Skyscapes." In her own artist's statement, she wrote, "The sky allows me to connect with feelings of wonder, passion, tragedy, and the sublime." Those large and lovely canvases now adorn the walls in my house and those of my two living brothers.

In her later years, my mother was softer and less critical, and thankfully by then I had also been able to validate my interests, talents, and skills. After her death, whatever it was that she and I used to argue about dissolved and disappeared. I could see clearly and admire fully the strong, accomplished, talented person she was, free of any power struggles between us.

What remains is the love. Actually, it was always about love. By now I have to really search my memory and work hard to even conjure up what any of our annoyances were.

As you read it, you will see that whatever her issues were with me, they too have fallen away. She does see me, after all.

Tears well up and my heart opens more every time I read this message from her. Since I am also a mother, I can totally relate to her comments about the miracle we each are, which is apparent from a child's first breath.

My dear Carol,

I have always loved you and all of my children beyond what I ever imagined my capacity for love could be. Each one of you added immeasurably to my experience of love… not by what you accomplished, but by your mere existence. That feeling of endless love came over me when you were each infants before you could have gone to any school or held any job. I experienced the miracle of each of you.

Growing up in my family, I have to say that I loved my father in that special way. However, I held everyone else, for various reasons, at something of an arm's distance. I was very intent on getting away from what I felt was the backward thinking of people in my family. I was afraid they would hold me back if I was too involved with them, and I pushed them away. I shut myself off from seeing their intrinsic beauty. I am not proud of this. I am also very grateful that I did break away.

Still, I was marked by the experiences of my upbringing, and I had many limitations. My fondest wish would be to erase any of the ways I may have passed on limitations to you. You can certainly give any of those negativities back to me…where I am they are instantly dis-integrated…no longer integrated! Yes! That is the key…dis-integrating anything, which does not serve the miracle of who you are.

Regrettably, societies…parents are included…foist all kinds of pressures and standards on others, which have the result of lessening one's miraculous self for the sake of approval and acceptance. You know I fell hard into many of these societal beliefs. I thought what I espoused was so much better than how I perceived the choices of my original family.

I did expand my horizons a great deal over the course of my life, but I also came to think that my way and your father's beliefs were the best, and you all should follow suit. What I was actually seeking was to help each of you to fulfill the wonderful uniqueness, which I saw in you when you were born. The motive was pure. Many of the methods were successful. Others, I am aware, were not.

I see now that somewhere along the line I inadvertently became a different version of my own parents, who assumed their ways were the best.

I admire you for learning over the course of your adult years how to not push your way onto anyone else. Rather, I can observe from my vantage point, how you help people clarify their ways. That frees up a lot of energy for everyone, and makes a lot more people happier!

I wish you and I could have seen eye-to-eye more often when I was alive. I saw a lot and had a lot inside that I could never articulate. I want you to remember the absolute love I have for you, and the beauty of who you are, which I saw the moment you were born, and which required NOTHING of you other than being there.

Please continue to help others reconnect with those inherent truths about themselves. The rest is all made-up stories. When people can see the miracle that they are, how wonderful everyone will feel and how nobly they will act.

Your Ole Mother

> *"What joy you bring me by living life*
> *on your own terms."*
> —Nina Shuman

Nina Shuman Loved Love

This letter is from Nina Shuman, the mother of one of my dear friends. The gentleness of her being and the joy she feels seeing her daughter, Laura, live a fulfilling life, emanate through her words. She passed away many years ago after a long illness.

Dearest Laura,

What joy you bring me by living life on your own terms. That is what you showed me, even when you were a little girl. I always admired your ability to know what you wanted and what you did not want.

You may have thought that I lived my life on my own terms, but really, I was an escapist. I only wanted to live in a beautiful, fairy tale world of love and beauty, with no sharp edges. In a sense, I never grew up. I lived for love, and I was very dependent on men to take away any worldly harshness. When I was in love and felt it was returned, I was like a flower in bloom. Being in love was always my intoxication.

I did things and moved through life looking very competent, but really I was only okay on the arm of my man. Thankfully, I was lucky in love.

But when it came to aging, and when I was faced with being old, and when in my fairy tale world there would be no more Prince Charming, I could not face that reality. Only now from my current perspective am I able to appreciate that I made the choice to die rather than face what I feared might be too much to endure.

This is why I so commend you and toast you because you are resourceful on your own. For you, a husband is frosting. This means you live a life more free and expansively than I ever could. I am so happy and proud you are my daughter.

With the exception of missing the chance to be with you and others in the family "in person," I am deliriously happy where I am. It is easier for me here. Life is softer. Love is more prevalent as part of the atmosphere here, so I feel bathed in love all the time.

I am very buoyant and also very steady, which is a combination I always sought, but did not often experience, in my time on Earth.

I have to tell you that I look young again as I did in the 1940s, when I felt most glamorous and the "world was my oyster." I am doing what you might call volunteer work. That's really a joke because there is no money here and no payment, regardless of what everyone does to contribute.

I make things beautiful. I work with flowers. I deck the halls. I sing for the happiness of others. I weave gorgeous tapestries with colors you don't even have where you are…and I can tell you that I do this without one iota of doubt about my competence. I am just being myself, living on my own terms and without any fear. I guess you could call it my version of heaven! Oh, and I can enjoy all the aspects of being myself, including my sense of humor. This is what I always wanted.

We are eternally linked in love. Why I have told you

all this is to cheer you on to live more the way I am able
to do here, right where you are and right now.
 All my love, and that's saying something!
 Your mother, Nina

"Dwelling on negative memories is useless.
Delete your 'complaint' files."
    −Betty Newman

____Betty Newman Offers Practical Pointers

Betty Newman was a tough, independent sort who lived in a small town in the Northwest. She shares a lot about the difference between surviving and thriving, wisdom for us all to take to heart.

Dear Joanne,

I was around all of you recently when you were all in the kitchen at Christmas time, did you notice? I so enjoyed when all of you shared fond memories about me.

Fond memories are like threads of love, which weave through your cells and create a fabric of love. My advice to you is to throw out all the rest. Dwelling on negative memories is useless. Delete all your "complaint" files. Having a lace-like net of love traveling with you at all times always helps and uplifts.

I managed to live a pretty long life. I had a "don't let the turkeys get you down" attitude for whatever and whoever ailed me. I was angry much of the time, which rallied my will to fight and to persevere. At the time, this was a perfect survival strategy. It allowed me to feel strong and to not be a victim when life and people would be oppressive. The attitude allowed me to feel I was taking charge in the face of serious difficulties.

However, I want you to know that I now understand that this strategy of mine was not about love. This was about using my will and a fight-back attitude to power my life. Don't get me wrong, it's a helpful attitude and sometimes totally appropriate, but it also got to be a habit to seek out opportunities to show the turkeys a thing or two. This is revenge, and the habit made it harder and harder to experience love in my life. I can see that it pushed all of you away.

I do not have regrets; I now see there is a step above survival, which is a better and more fulfilling way to live. Only now do I realize that I can turn around the habit of living "on guard." Instead of looking out for all the turkeys, I can have a new habit, which is to attract the good guys and see what's good in people and in life.

The reason I can understand all this is because nothing bad or mean happens here, so I finally got to push the "at-ease" and the "down-girl" switches.

You get the drift. I hope all that I am learning gives you a window into me to understand me better. Perhaps you can now let go of the ways I may have hurt you by my tough-love survival mode of living.

It is also meant to be a pointer for you so that you can drop whatever you may have learned by my example of living life through a veil of complaints. I know you concern yourself with the sorry state of the world and what you might contribute. Please keep in mind that fighting the turkeys may not always be the best strategy.

Finally, I know you wonder how you ever ended up with me as your mother. Though it was not possible while I was with you to experience me as a deep thinker and someone who seeks answers to the mysteries of life…we do share this passion. I was, and you are (more successfully) exploring how to get out of fear. I am so happy that

you are already so much farther along in your life than
I could have ever been.

Always focus on what is right about your life. That
viewpoint will make you happy.

I love you always, Mother

*"My soul is always my soul, and all the experiences
of my soul are forever recorded."*
—Mary Marcus

___Mary Marcus Has Big News

Mary adores her three adult daughters and is so happy to tell them about what's next for her. In this Transmission, she also answers the frequently asked question: "If my mother reincarnates, can I still communicate with her?"

My Dear Missy, Sally, and Jodie,

It is so wonderful to be communicating with you, and how special that you are all together. This makes a mother's heart rejoice.

I have something exciting to tell you right away. This will boggle your brilliant minds. I am getting ready to reincarnate again, and I know I will be a baby girl!

Needless to say, I am very excited. Most people have only taken the time to wonder what it is like to die. (I'll tell you all about that part in a moment.) But, how many people ever consider what it is like to be born? I completely trust how and when this will happen. Right now, I do not know any more specifics. However, dying was a completely natural process, so being born will be so, too.

Before you freak out worrying that you'll never be able to communicate with me again, let me set this straight. My soul is always my soul and all the experiences of my soul are forever recorded. One of my soul's identities was as your mother. You can always reach me by calling in your mother, and you can contact me anytime because souls are not subject to time or space. In fact, you could look into the records of my soul in what you'd call my past lives, and eventually, you can peek into my future incarnation.

As I promised, here is a quick rundown of events related to dying. The mind puts endless energy into what it will be like to die. The emotions conjure up all kinds of dramas and fears about dying. The physical body does its best to keep on surviving. After all the effort, when the time comes, the body automatically knows what to do to shut itself down. The soul knows how to release itself seamlessly from the body.

There is sort of a twilight zone where the soul's awareness floats in and out of the old body, which allows the orientation to the new, less physically dense body to occur. When someone familiar would speak, there was an immediate focus back into the physical body. Then consciousness drifts away to the new form and resumes getting adjusted there.

Somehow there is also an "observer" part of the self, which watches this flow toward transitioning and fully understands the process. I guess an analogy is how you can be having a dream, and without ever waking up, another part of yourself lets you know, "Oh, this is only a dream."

At the time of death, there is a burst of light, and you just step out like you are walking out of one room and into another, and you are in a different reality.

I continue to think and to experience my five senses. There are people in the new reality whom I have not met before, and those who are familiar. Everything is so much *lighter; not only because you have a healthy body again, but also because you have taken off all kinds of stuff you've been dragging around in the life just completed. It feels great; everyone is met, welcomed, and oriented.*

You have already heard that what you think happens immediately here. I always loved Hawaii, so I zoom over there on purpose at times. It does require carefully managing one's thoughts. The same is true in your Earth lives as well. You are less aware of how powerful your thoughts are because it takes longer for things to show up.

In my life I did always try, not always successfully, to measure my words, and to think good thoughts to maintain a level of inner peace. What I experience here is the ultimate of that. It's so important to never throw away words.

You can tell that I am very happy, and I am just overflowing with feelings of love for all of you, along with a sense of fulfillment within myself.

What I would convey to each one of you is to please make certain that you do in your lives what gives you real joy. I mean not just a drop of pure joy here and there, or even a teaspoonful every now and then. I am talking about a lifestyle of joy…expressing loving kindness wherever you go and sharing the gifts of your talents.

Your generation of women is freer than mine was. I always struggled to be valued as an equal with my mate, and I was burdened with societal notions of "the good wife" and "the good mother" and "the good person in the community."

Truth is, in those days, the word "good" meant that you didn't cause any waves to disturb the men, and in my generation, we all said a silent "yes" to all that silliness and reined in our fullest potential. Now it is just good humor to reflect on all this. I feel so blessed to know so much more now.

My cup runneth over; I love you each so much, and I am always and forever,

Your Mother

P.S. If it is appropriate, please let dad know that living life on Earth is the hard part. Tell him I love him, and that all else is long ago taken by the wind.

> *"The postmark on these Transmissions*
> *will read: 'The Other Side!'"*
> — Natasha Lee

___Natasha Lee Prefers Postcards

Here was a surprise. This Transmission came in the format of postcards, which Anna and Lori's mother wanted to use for her messages to her grown daughters. In this first postcard she describes how groups of souls on the other side together create the realities they live in. This concept of co-creating our reality has potential application to our lives. In the second postcard, enjoy what she has to say about soul mates.

POSTCARD NO. 1:

Dear wonderful daughters of mine,

I have always liked postcards, and would like to consider this the first in a series of postcards from me to all of you. The postmark will read: "The Other Side!"

I live in a beautiful place in the reality you call the "Other Side." This lovely landscape is something a group of us here, who are on the same learning level, are creating as a "class project." As a group, we have developed a vision for a geography in which we would like to live. By the power of our thoughts, the energy of the shared vision has created our little geography.

There are green rolling hills, trees, flowers, ponds and lakes, birds, and a temperate climate. We all chose to avoid extremes in weather, and we all enjoy gorgeous sunsets. For this project to succeed, we all have to maintain the focus on the creation we are collectively projecting. If someone drops the focus, it shows immediately because either we get some bad weather or parts of our natural surroundings start disappearing. We automatically see who needs help getting back on track so they can resume contributing the energy of their thoughts back into our matrix.

We won't be living in this place forever, but you can see that we are mastering the impact of our individual thoughts, the power of a group vision and how to maintain that focus.

Since you help business teams to create a group vision and a shared culture, I am hoping what I have described can be useful. Obviously, thoughts manifest more slowly on the Earth plane, but there is a definite correlation with how Earth realities are created both on an individual and group basis.

I will send out more postcards soon. I love each of you, and it is a relief to say so with such uncomplicated conviction.

Your Mother

> *"Unconditional love is not a fantasy."*
> —Natasha Lee

POSTCARD NO. 2:

Dear Anna and Lori,

This is so much fun and so gratifying; I am so happy that I am singing.

You have asked me a question about love and soul mates.

Whenever anyone has that special, immediate, and mutual heart connection with another person, there is a soul connection. Why? The human heart is the portal to the soul. From my point of observation, to call someone a soul mate means you have both decided to nourish and support that heart/soul connection. If you choose to become partners in life, then you are literally soul mates.

People on Earth give too much weight to the term "soul mate." Any relationship where there is unconditional love is a soul-based experience. This is a good thing.

Unconditional love is not a fantasy. It is the experience of the soul overflowing through your heart. The soul naturally accepts all parts of the other person.

I will send another postcard soon. Do you have more questions?

Your Mother

*"Please tell 'our' son that being loyal to me
would mean for him to live a happy life."*
—Martha, our son's birth mother

____Deceased Birth Mother Offers Insights

Jeanne Doyle is the mother of an adopted son, whose biological mother, Martha, died before Jeanne could find her. Jeanne wanted to communicate with her adopted son's deceased biological mother. This is an example of an extraordinary collaboration, not only between a biological mother and an adoptive mother, but also between the living and someone on the other side. Both mothers were so grateful for this opportunity to work together for the good of their child.

Dear adoptive mother of our son,

My heart has been softened being where I am now, so I can say that your interest in me, and what I might have to say to our son, who is truly your son, warms my heart. Most of my life, I felt that things were too much to bear and that life must not be on my side. So, I often acted tough and hard-hearted. Inside that was not the case, but not many knew that.

I have died young as the result of building walls around my heart. The first thing I would tell our son is that no matter what life dishes up, do not harden your heart. It really does not work as a strategy. It makes things worse.

I would also tell him that thinking of life as endless struggles and as a series of impossible hurdles to overcome is a foolish way to live. I know this from sorry experience. In case this view of life is genetic, I wanted you to know how I used to relate to my life.

From what I can understand now, life is meant to be about positive things and joy. Our son can choose whatever view of life he wants, but please tell him to be careful what he chooses because he will then live it. You are definitely showing him that life is uplifting and full of possibilities.

But I do think that, like me, he works from a certain "one down" place. I am told that people who are adopted are loyal to their birth parents, even though they may never see them after being born. This is a spooky thing, but I assure you, it is so.

Please tell him that being loyal to me would mean to live a happy life.

It is hard for any child who is adopted to really believe in their heart that they were not abandoned or rejected. I can tell you this is also a biological thing...it sounds crazy, but cells "recognize" the cells of their own biological parents. Even if a child never is told he or she is adopted, something in their biology "knows."

I hope that with all I am sharing with you, it will be possible for you to explain a lot to our son. My wish for him, with all my heart, is to have a positive view of himself and of all life. He would not have been exposed to that opportunity through me. He needed to be with you for that part.

His fate was to come from me and to learn through you. This is actually amazing me as I am telling you all this. Truly, your request for information is helping me understand so much more about myself, too. It is a healing for me.

If our son wants to practice loyalty, then this is it. Here is the ultimate: Be loyal to the amazing gifts life has to offer. The best I had to give was to see to it he had a chance this could be true for him.

Tell him I love him and that I will always help him from my position in this other reality. This is how my role can be positive and constant and pure.

Thank you again. I must withdraw now and follow my thoughts to other places.

Your grateful co-parent, Martha

> *"At first I thought, 'Who will I be without*
> *my history of struggles?'"*
> −Jane Anderson

___Jane Discovers Suffering is Optional

Jane Anderson was a single mother of two boys, and she had many personal challenges in her life. She shares with her now-adult sons how she burdened her heart during her life, which she now sees as optional suffering. She wants her sons to benefit from her experience and to practice forgiveness. Her joy in being free from those limitations serves as an inspiration to live in literally a more lighthearted way.

> *My dear Michael and Steven,*
>
> *I know that a more correct format for this letter would be to open with a chatty preamble, but I would rather get right to my message, and I assure you that I am fine.*
>
> *Soon after arriving here, there is the phase of reviewing the life I just completed...not at all as I might have expected...in terms of successes and failures, but in terms of rebalancing the heart. We get to see all the burdens we carry in our hearts...burdens created from accumulated fears, frustrations, lack of self-worth, hurts, grudges, judgments, and limiting beliefs.*
>
> *The atmosphere of total love makes it possible to look at myself without defending anything or being self-critical. Reviewing my life objectively and compassionately allows me to let go of my heart burdens. At first I was afraid to do this. I thought, "Who will I be without my history of*

struggles?" I got to press the "delete" key with an effortless tap, one former weight on the heart at a time.

And voila, each weight is lifted off of my heart, and here is the best part: As each burden is released, old illnesses, distresses, and unhappiness disappear. Now this is my kind of house cleaning! It is such a good feeling, I am telling you, and it's a delicious experience to feel so light and joyful.

From our vantage point, we see all of you who are still alive, not in terms of your daily joys and pains or even your specific struggles and pleasures. We see into your hearts and notice if your heart has become heavy in the presence of all that life serves up.

We here do our very best to help loosen the edges of anything that is weighing on your hearts. That is my current "job."

There are large numbers of us here who are eager to assist you if you ask. It requires your permission. Our help is unconditional, which means that we are not at all frustrated if one of you immediately re-creates your heart burdens. It is a joy to not be controlling anymore.

Because I experienced a lot of hurt in my life, I know I was overly sensitive to little things. You may not have been aware of the depths to which I used to suffer anytime someone didn't like a meal I prepared or rejected an idea of mine or cast a glance that I interpreted as disapproving. By taking everything personally, I suffered. This is how I managed to continue accumulating so much weight on my heart.

I want you to know that what counts most toward a person's health and happiness is forgiving the things that weigh down the heart. I certainly did not manage that form of lightness of being in my life. The triumph is practicing this in your world.

As your mother, I believe in you both, and my wish is for your life to be much better than mine. What I hope is that in addition to meeting life's challenges, you also extend to yourself the loving compassion to unburden your heart after each difficulty.

A human heart can always forgive and remain pure. It is a choice. This wisdom is the treasure I have learned since my passing.

I admire you beyond your knowing. God bless you. The simple truths I have shared with you in this letter are the true race for the cure.

Thank you so much for wanting to contact me.

I love you always, Mom

Pearls of Wisdom

Unconditional love is the universal, underlying experience of parenthood. Sometimes personal issues and the stresses of daily life can cloud this pure love, but at the soul level, it is always there. Whether or not you have lost your mother, please take comfort from these Transmissions in knowing that no matter how close or how complicated your relationships are or have been, unconditional love prevails.

"*That feeling of endless love came over me when you were each infants before you could have gone to any school or held any job. I experienced the miracle of each of you...When people can see the miracle that they are, how wonderful everyone will feel and how nobly they will act.*" –Ida Mann

"*We are eternally linked in love. Why I have told you all of this is to cheer you on to live [from love]...right where you are and right now. All my love, and that's saying something!*" –Nina

"*I hope all I am learning gives you a window into me to understand me better. Perhaps you can now let go of the ways I may have hurt you by my tough-love survival mode of living. Dwelling on negative memories is useless. Delete your 'complaint' files.*" –Betty

"*You can always reach me by calling in your mother, and you can contact me anytime because souls are not subject to time or space.*" –Mary

"*Unconditional love is not a fantasy. It is the experience of the soul overflowing through your heart.*" –Natasha

"*The first thing I would tell our son is that no matter what life dishes up, do not harden your heart.*" –Martha

"*I want you to know that what counts most toward a person's health and happiness is forgiving the things that weigh down the heart. A human heart can always forgive...it is a choice.*" –Jane

___Why Wait Meditation: Making Lemonade to Support Your Evolution

There is an important and often-overlooked opportunity to feel gratitude and to take positive action about what we perceive our mothers were not able to express or to give us. We have the choice to turn anything we wish our mothers had done more of or less of, into what will make us better people.

○ *Create a quiet moment and reflect on a trait or traits you wish your mother had more of or less of, had she been, in your estimation, a more perfect mother for you.*

○ *Next, "freeze frame" this list in your mind, as if you paused a DVD.*

○ *Focus your awareness now on your own heart, and take three more deep, slow breaths.*

○ *Take the following perspective into your heart. This trait or these traits you have identified are precisely what you are meant to cultivate in yourself this life.*

○ *Be with this new awareness.*

○ *Open your eyes.*

○ *Enjoy the new perspective and the accompanying knowledge and feeling of self-empowerment.*

Chapter 4

Transmissions from Fathers to Their Children

THE FIRST THEME in these Transmissions is that fathers, like mothers, unanimously express their abiding love for their families. They share the heartfelt desire that their loved ones find happiness in their lives. From the expanded awareness of the afterlife, these men encourage us to find happiness on our own terms, a far cry from their egos dictating what they considered to be the right way to live, the right person to marry, or the right job to hold.

Speaking from their soulful selves with so much less ego interference and no societal pressures, these men also share personal insights about what mattered most in their lives and troubling things they often kept to themselves or were not even aware of until they passed. Not surprisingly, their professional lives dominated their attention, and many of these men express regret at not being more openly affectionate with their family members. Their advice to us is to say the words, "I love you," often and to literally reach out and touch people as another way to consistently communicate that invaluable message.

You might notice, as do I, that there is more awareness and joy expressed in the Transmissions because there is less input from the ego and more soul presence. Clearly, retiring from the ego-driven life without dying to accomplish this, is an important takeaway for us to experience lasting fulfillment and inner peace in our lives. Hopefully, like me, you are inspired to practice putting the ego in the passenger's seat as consistently as possible right here and now.

One simple way to have less ego interference is to recognize when that part of the self is running your life. Ego urges always feel needy, insistent, and whiney. The ego is the part of us that is always comparing and contrasting, judging, and always taking everything personally. Once you are familiar with the ego's repertoire, you can choose to indulge it or to override it. I like to think of the ego as the fear-based relative of the soul. Putting the soul in the driver's seat of our lives leads to more lasting fulfillment.

Enjoy these letters full of wisdom, wit, and more information for us to apply to our lives here and now.

"I am not so far away, and yet I cannot
just reach out and touch you."
–Martin Sulzberg

____Martin Assures His Daughter

Martin Sulzberg perished in the crash of a private plane. He shares his experience during and after the crash in clear and simple language, reassuring his daughter, Ellie, that he is okay and learning with others about how to navigate in their new reality.

Dearest Ellie,

You are tormenting yourself wondering what my experience was when the plane crashed. Here it is, and I am fine, so please put your heart at ease.

We were told that the plane was having mechanical difficulties, and we were going to make an unscheduled landing. It was night so you couldn't see anything out the window, and there were no inside lights either.

This was the only time I was afraid. I had that in-stantaneous…oh my God, this is serious…maybe this is it…sort of feeling, which ran through my body like cold electricity. I muttered some sort of prayer like, "Please God, let this plane be safe." And then my thoughts were not focused on anything…time was suspended hoping and waiting to be told more or to know by the sounds that we were able to make a safe landing.

There was silence in the plane. I wasn't panicked. I assumed the crew was handling the mechanical problems.

The next thing I knew, I was floating in the air looking down at the wreck of our plane. It was silent and peaceful where we were. Debris was everywhere on the ground below.

This was when it occurred to me for the first time that we had crashed. Just as I began to wonder what was going on…there were people coming to greet us. There were people coming from all directions; there was someone for each of us who had been on the plane.

My parents met me and were so happy to see me. They looked so young that I was confused. I was thinking, "What are you doing here, and how can you be so young?" I was trying to figure it all out. At the same time, I was overwhelmed with their love. This was a giant love-in.

My parents told me what had happened, and that everyone would be taken to a place to rest and recuperate. My parents were escorting me there. It seemed oddly normal to me, and I relaxed in their company. I was still disoriented, but I felt safe and taken care of. This is the best I can explain it.

Whenever I think about you, I can immediately see you and whatever you are doing. I am not so far away, and yet I cannot just reach out and touch you. Mostly, I am very busy with orientation and learning the way things function. There are others here who are in the same boat as me…I would say I am in a group of average learners when it comes to mastering all this.

You have to be very slow and steady with thinking and moving here, or it's chaotic. This reminds me of all my not-so-steady, hand-held home videos, which would always make everyone watching them feel dizzy! I am sure that I will master this. Everyone *does, and everyone is 100% supportive.*

So, my dear, I hope this begins to let you know about my situation. No need to worry anymore. I am fine, and by the way, my "classmates" are envious that I am communicating with you.

With deep love, I am always, Your Father

"Does this mean I am now some enlightened man?
Nope. It only means that I have one big insight."
—Judd Cedarholm

___Bob Introduces His Father, Judd, Who Tells It Like He Sees It

My father was a "Marlboro Man." He was born, lived, and worked all his life amid the mountains and wide-open spaces of Montana. He could ride and pack any horse, fight forest fires, fix plumbing, build furniture, sew his own work pants, and fix all our toys. I remember him as a strong silent presence, but always ready with a quick joke and a one-liner. He was a "man's man," who only opened up after a few whiskeys in the bar with his few male friends. He could cook anything in a skillet, and fried us eggs and bacon for breakfast practically every morning of our childhood.

What struck me immediately when I received the Transmission from my father, a few years after his death, was the metaphor he used for how our beliefs are unraveled on the other side. "It comes loose like scraping the bottom of a frying pan." This metaphor was definitely something my father knew well...and Carol Mann did not know...from all his years of camp cooking and making us breakfast. There were also words in the Transmission like "chuckle" and "nope" that my father used frequently in his life. The tone of the message is also true to my father. He was a man who withheld his feelings and kept everything inside, never showing easy affection to anyone. He had a huge heart that never got to really open.

Before receiving the Transmission, I had hopes that I would finally hear my father say that he loved me, and that would make my relationship with him complete. So, it was a surprise that the most powerful line for me in the Transmission was when he said, "...No one here wants me to be other than how I am." His comment struck at the heart of a painful theme that has run in our family line, perhaps for generations—that we're not enough and need to continually try to change that status. It was very poignant to hear him express that he is free of this family issue, which I know plagued him.

My mother always thought that dad could have done better if only he'd gotten a college education, if only we had more money, if only...then life would be better. I have also struggled with feeling that I am not enough, and I see so clearly where I learned this. It now stands out like a flashing neon sign, how holding this belief about oneself and about life is a guaranteed prescription for never being happy with who you are or grateful for what you have.

At some level, I always knew that my dad loved us. Now I know that he is finally finding some peace. Thankfully, I continue to make great progress in breaking the family pattern by appreciating who I am and treasuring all that I have been blessed with in my life.
    —Bob Cedarholm

To my son, Bob,

This is a memo from your father:

To answer your question, I am okay, and everyone on this side is okay because there is no hell. Hell is on Earth, and is composed of what people say and do to each other and to themselves.

On this side, everyone gets to unravel all of that. It comes loose like scraping the bottom of a frying pan. Some pans have less stuck to them, so they come clean easier and quicker than others. The spatula is simply the atmosphere here. There is no resistance, so things don't stick.

I know you are already chuckling because I was the former king of resistance, stubbornness, and other sticky wickets, and I took pride in that. I enjoyed being the guy looking down his nose, and I liked saying, "Nope," to something others would ask me to do. I was the guy of few words when others wanted to talk, and I teased people often to see them squirm.

Now, all joking aside, this way of mine, the perverse pleasure in saying no and denying people what they needed, got to be a big problem for me. Over the decades, I lost the ability to even guess what others needed from me, and I felt I had nothing to offer.

You are smart enough to see that anyone who so proudly builds emotional walls actually creates their own prison and becomes the prisoner.

So, now the walls are starting to come down, and my prison is rapidly disappearing. Does that mean the prisoner goes free and runs around happy, full of love and is miraculously a new person? No, it means the guy stands there without the walls.

When I stand "naked" here, no one ever jeers or makes fun of me. So, I stand without my walls and get to observe how I do that negativity to myself. Then after some time watching the self-flagellation, the "aha" begins to creep in and to take hold. So, the "aha" turns into a "ha ha ha ha," a big laugh. The joke is on me. I see what I did to myself my whole life.

Does this mean I am now some enlightened man?

Nope, it only means that I have one big insight. After that, we shall see what's next.

To your "Did I love you?" question, here is the answer for right now. I said to myself all my life that I loved all my children and your mother. At the time, I had no idea what that meant or what that felt like. How could I? I was so shut down all the time. Saying that I loved all of you out loud seemed unnecessary. I knew I loved all of you, and that was enough for me. Your mother was deep and had complex emotions, not me.

I like it here. I like being out of my Earth "hell." It is a relief and relaxing. There are no chores and no demands, and no one needs me to be other than how I am.

I really did like being your father. You have always had great spunk, which I admire. You were always refreshing. I always knew you would go far. I knew this meant you would move far away from home, and that you would do well in whatever you did. Keep going—you have a lot to contribute.

With love from your father, who is not in heaven and not in hell, and that is just fine by me.

Dad

"No one seems aware of my presence when I still pop into your reality now and then to check on you all. But there is one exception: The dogs can see me."
– George Madden

Rejuvenated George Shares a Regret

George Madden died at age 97 and is thrilled to have a younger body now that he is on the other side. As he writes to his son, William, you'll also hear one of the repeating themes from fathers: He regrets not having expressed his love more freely during his life. This is an easy one for us to correct right now.

Dear William,

The best thing about my new experience is that I am young and nimble, and I don't have to deal with that old, creaky body. My mind thankfully stayed more or less intact to the end, but that body....

After dying, I had such a sense of relief to not be hauling around my old bones. I was immediately rejuvenated, not exactly kicking up my heels, but intact and feeling good. I was met not only by people I had known, but also by a noticeable sense of inner peace. The reunions and the relaxation were a wonderful combination.

Dying is not traumatic. Thinking about leaving you all and the world I had grown to love is the hard part. The actual moment of dying is similar to how smooth it is to lie down at night and without knowing the exact moment, you just fall asleep. Only I am not at all asleep; I am just making that comparison. Another analogy is that death is like flying from one city to another. You leave the city you are in that is full of familiar sounds, sights, people, and places, and you step off the plane into another city, which is equally full of life, but is less familiar.

And then I realized that I was somewhere else, and not with you. This is hard for me still. I can see and hear each of you. I have been by your mother's side often. No one seems aware of my presence when I still pop into your reality to check on you all every now and then. But there is one exception: The dogs can see me. I am hoping that someday you will also sense my presence. I put my hand on your shoulder often.

I have a bunch of small regrets about my life, but there is one big one: It's that I did not talk enough about what I liked while I was alive, and I did not tell you and your mother how much I loved you. I complained a lot; I was quick to voice my objections…okay, I was downright opinionated about everyone and everything.

I want you to know that you have always been the apple of my eye. I am your dad who will always love you. I always treasured your mother, too. I wanted you to know that.

*"What is important is to find a shortcut to remind
you of your true loving nature so you can rekindle it
in the midst of life's ups and downs."*
—Ernesto Sanchez

Maria's Father Shares His Secret to Life

Dearest Maria,

*I am aware of the many questions you have about
my life. Here is one I would like to answer right now.
You have been wondering: What was the secret to my
ability to be calm and steady in my love for everyone in
the family, even when things were difficult?*

*I had a little trick, which made this possible. When
each of you kids was little, I made it a point to come
into your room after you were asleep. I would gaze at
each of you in wonderment. What I saw and felt was
the exquisite purity of your souls. I always kept that
close to my heart.*

*Whenever I would lose my inner equilibrium at
work or at home...whenever I was about to clutter my
mind with judgments and criticisms, I would bring to
mind the image of my children as you slept. This would
quickly remind me that every person has that purity in
them somewhere. This point of view would smooth me
out almost immediately.*

*This trick of mine might not work for you, but I
am sure you can find something equivalent to use for
yourself. What is important is to find a shortcut, which
reminds you of your true loving nature, so that you can
quickly rekindle it in the midst of life's ups and downs.*

As far as I can observe, when you think of me, your

heart opens no matter what else might be preoccupying you. So, without too much of a pat on my back, maybe I can be the love equilibrium trick for you as you have been for me.

Your loving Papa

> *"I have a 'job' here as part of a group assisting*
> *parents who are alive on the Earth to nurture*
> *their children's natural talents."*
>
> – George Brier

____George's Work in the Afterlife is a Healing

George Brier was the product of his generation, where the man's role was to support the family. Locked into that stereotype, he now sees he lacked the inclination to move beyond the prescribed role to spend time with his children when they were growing up. This is a reminder to be mindful of any "roles" we take on so that they do not limit us unnecessarily. A course correction for him is that his work in the spirit world is to help parents be more supportive and loving with their children.

Dear Family,

I have been feeling very shy about making this communication. I prefer that my life be like water under the bridge, which flows into the sea and disperses completely. Hey! That line just surprised me…it is rather poetic.

I am peaceful here. Even when I look at my life and notice it was mainly filled with a lot of work and routines. I was not an original; I did not show much emotion, and I would rate my life as average. I was living the roles of provider, husband, and father. I knew little about parenting.

In my day, the father earned the living and touched in briefly with the kids. The mother did everything else. I am neither proud nor self-recriminating about this. It is just what it was, and I did my best. When I look at my recent life it is like watching an old-time movie... everything is dated...somewhat charming and not very deep...very dated.

I have a "job" here as part of a group assisting parents who are alive on the Earth to nurture their children's natural talents. We don't intervene, but we can "whisper" guidance by literally suggesting things, which the person might then feel as "a sudden inspiration." We don't always get through to the parents, but we never tire or get frustrated. We enjoy finding new ways to nudge them. The total lack of impatience is such a wonderful thing and a relief for me. I always had high expectations for myself and was rarely satisfied. I blamed myself, but can see that I often took it out on everyone else.

I am so happy that you have such a long life ahead of you. I love you, and I will continue to love you. I thank you for your love in spite of my shortcomings.

Now that I have finally communicated, I hesitate to close. Sounds like the story of my old life. First, he wasn't sure he wanted to stay. Then, he hated to leave.

At least I still have a sense of humor, and I can wholeheartedly say, "I love you."

"It only occurred to me after dying that my life-long negative attitude, somewhat hidden by my wit, was like shoveling dirt on my own grave."

–Ken Gold

___Ken Shares the Flip Side of His Sense of Humor

Ken Gold's long and ultimately fatal illness wore him out and robbed him of his funny side, which he is so happy to reclaim. His letter reveals important insight about what was underneath all the joking around in his life. It is an opportunity to consider what motivates your particular kind of humor.

My dear children,

Here's a good one! If I could sing, it would be, "The world is alive"...because I can see the aliveness in everything and in everyone so clearly where I am. I realize this sounds ridiculous and corny coming from me, but I want to tell you that I can look at a person and see the aliveness pouring out of their skin! This is all very exhilarating, like champagne bubbles. It is so uplifting.

It does me so much good to regain some of my zest. Oh, how I regretted losing that and feeling like a stick in the mud. I am now lighthearted, and so is everyone here who has been, at one time or another, referred to as "the dearly departed."

It is okay to be dearly departed from having a heavy heart, a heavy body, and carrying heavy emotional weight, as well. My version was that life had gotten me down. I had such a bad attitude and took everything I was asked to do or to be in life as another weight piled on. It only occurred to me after dying that my negative attitude, somewhat hidden by my wit, was like shoveling dirt on my own grave.

Underneath my external funny side, I was sad a lot of my life. I was always keeping a relatively stiff upper lip…but I was taking it in the hip and in joints and wherever it was possible to get stiff.

I know I may sound like someone who has gone off the deep end, but I already did that during my life on Earth. This is the other side, and for me, it is a delight.

Please know that I love you always and forever, no matter what you choose to do or not to do in your life. Please love yourself in that same way. You already know, from my less-than-fabulous example, that having a negative attitude and also covering that up with being a witty stoic does not make for health or happiness. Please be happy, and love yourself. Your good health will follow!

Always and forever, Your Father

"The most important thing I can tell you
is you were conceived in love."

___Marci Introduces Her Biological Father who Offers Healing

I was adopted at birth. I never met my biological father, and I was not able to locate him before he died. I have known Carol for a dozen years and had many special readings from her prior to being brave enough to ask for this Transmission from my deceased father, whom I never knew.

Many years ago, I had found and met my birth mother, and sadly discovered very little connection with her, so I wasn't sure I was emotionally ready to reach out for any type of connection to my biological father.

This Transmission from him was a blast of sunshine for me. The very first sentence, "You were conceived in love," released the fear from my heavy heart and gave me an overwhelming feeling of gratitude.

My father's description of how he was parented, the restrictions placed on him, and his thoughts about parenting all ring loudly in my ears. He has given a beautiful reminder for me as a parent to create a space and provide fertile ground for my children to develop their own ideas and forge their own paths and identities, where they (as my father stated in his Transmission to me) "may be free to live their dreams, to be happy and to have it all."

His letter was comforting to me on so many levels. I relate to the struggles he spoke of, especially his quest for the idyllic life and his struggle to make his overachieving and ambitious parents happy with his personal life choices. Sadly, in order to please them, he was not true to his own heart.

My takeaway message from this letter is to follow my heart, living my life to the fullest on my terms with respect and compassion for others.

I also love what he says about a world with NO WARS, and that someday love will be considered the most important thing in all relationships. I was born in 1964.

−Marcie Roberts

My dear daughter,

The most important thing I can tell you is you were conceived in love. I was a very romantic guy in my day, and I was in love with your mother.

In the old movie version of South Pacific, *there is a love scene on the beach of a tropical island. Your mother was my exotic beauty, and I would often think of us as if we were in that film. What is a fantasy, anyway? What is love, anyway? It is a feeling evoked from the inside of a person. Does it matter in the moment if that love is forever in the form of marriage?*

My love at that time was real for your mother, and I can say that she also loved me…but we were both living in denial about how it could turn out. I was not courageous enough at the time to challenge my parents' requirement to marry someone of the same faith and ethnic background. They would have disowned me, and I lacked the guts to face the shame of being ousted. In a crazy way, your existence is the only proof that our love was real. All the rest is now invisible.

Please understand that I do not recommend living

in denial, or on fantasies, for that matter. Fooling oneself in terms of what is really possible never works out well. However, without dreams, nothing ever advances, does it? That idealistic shortcoming of mine allowed me the fleeting feeling of a perfect love in an ideal world, which was always something I wanted to experience, and I never did in a long-term relationship.

I worked hard and played hard, and pushed myself and was pushed by my family to succeed and to excel... you know, to have it all, to be it all. There is nothing wrong with this kind of parenting; I guess it is another kind of ideal...but what it never allowed me to acknowledge in myself was the soft, poetic kind of guy. I was sort of like the knight from the Middle Ages who had to go to war to prove himself to family, country, and God, when all he wanted was to live with his "lady love" and have a normal life. Romantic, idealized love or breaking any norm was in great contrast to how I grew up.

So, I was a dreamer and a scientist. What a funny combination. I was both. Did I have regrets in my life? Yes. Would I have done anything differently? I did not feel that I could in that life, but in the next one, you bet! Show me the chance to live in a world where you can have breakthroughs in every aspect of life...to love anyone you want no matter who that is, to create whatever career you want as long as it involves breakthroughs, which help people, and of course time to play (more physical breakthroughs), and I am there! Oh, and no wars.

Am I aware of you? Yes. It will sound strange, but souls on the other side can search for any living person they choose. We do not and cannot interfere, and I did *search for you and find you. For me, you represent the new generation, the new blend, and a new world without boundaries, where hopefully, soon love will prevail in all ways.*

Be free, be happy, and may you have it all; however you define that for yourself. Please know that you were conceived in love. Not everyone is conceived with that gift.

___Pearls of Wisdom

These fathers are so caring as they each offer their version of "a full situation report" to their children. They tell what it is like to die, what they are doing on the other side, add comforting assurances they are doing well and let us know they love us forever.

"Mostly I am very busy with orientation and learning the way things function here. There are others here who are in the same boat as me...I would say I am in a group of average learners when it comes to mastering all this. Everyone does, and everyone is 100% supportive." –Martin

"To answer your question, I am okay, and everyone on this side is okay because there is no hell. Hell is on Earth and is composed of what people say and do to each other and to themselves...I like it here...no one needs me to be other than how I am." –Judd

"Another analogy is that death is like flying from one city to another. You leave the city you are in that is full of familiar sights, sounds, people, and places, and you step off the plane into another city, which is equally full of life, but it is less familiar." –George

"What is important is to find a shortcut, which reminds you of your true loving nature, so that you can quickly rekindle it in the midst of life's ups and downs. When each of you were kids, I made it a point to come into your room after you were asleep. I would gaze at each of you in wonderment. I always kept that close to my heart. This point of view would smooth me out immediately." –Ernesto

"I have a 'job' here as part of a group assisting parents who are alive on the Earth to nurture their children's natural talents... We don't always get through to the parents, but we never tire or get frustrated." –George B.

"Please know I love you forever, no matter what you choose to do or not to do in your life. Please be happy, and love yourself. Your good health will follow!" –Ken

"For me, you represent the new generation, the new blend, and a new world without boundaries, where hopefully, love will prevail in all ways." –Marci's biological dad

___Why Wait Meditation: Finding a Shortcut to What Really Matters

Ernesto has great advice to his daughter about the importance of having a "shortcut" for connecting with what really matters in life in the face of daily stresses and distractions. Here's an exercise to connect with your heart and create your own shortcut.

○ *Take a few moments to sit comfortably in a quiet place, close your eyes, and take a few deep, relaxing breaths.*

○ *Focus your awareness on your physical heart.*

○ *Keeping your eyes closed, imagine you can literally breathe in and out of your heart.*

○ *As you continue to imagine inhaling and exhaling through your heart, bring to mind a person or a pet that you cherish more than anything.*

○ *Feel the love spread through your entire body.*

○ *Gently open your eyes. Notice how you now feel.*

○ *Use this shortcut any time you lose sight of what really matters.*

Chapter 5

Transmissions from Friends to Friends

AS YOU WILL READ in these Transmissions, a treasured friend is literally forever. These friends continue to share confidences, offer support, cheer us on and even say they periodically check in on us to continue enjoying our presence. They emphasize that they are always only a heartfelt thought away, and will always assist us if we ask.

Often the only way friends on the other side can contact us is when we are asleep and dreaming. In that state, we are free of the distractions of daily life, the mind chatter is still, and our consciousness can be more aware of interacting with other dimensions of reality. The analogy is that the stars are always there, but we cannot see them in the daytime. Our souls are always capable of perceiving things beyond our five senses; however, those experiences cannot easily get through the filter of everyday activities and concerns.

There are ways to connect with friends on the other side when we are awake. It requires being still, asking from and listening with the heart rather than the head. The meditation at the end of this chapter is designed to guide you in doing this.

*"My body may have been dysfunctional, and I did not have
the brain coherence to communicate, but my consciousness
was clear, and I was able to perceive everything."*
—Esther Forman

Esther's Passing was Eased by the Presence of Friends

Esther Forman died in her thirties and was blessed with
a circle of lifelong special women friends who supported her in every step along her journey with cancer. As
you will read, they followed her wishes and helped her
to conclude her life with dignity. She felt there must be
something wrong with her that she did not beat cancer.
In fact, part of her new awareness is that her entire life
she operated from the belief there was something in-
herently "wrong" with her. She now knows that was not
true. Hopefully, she inspires anyone who also thinks
they are "flawed" to let go of this untruth right now.

> *Dear best girlfriends,*
> *Where to start…*
> *There was such a sense of peace when you surrounded
> me at the end of my life. By then, it was not about recogniz-
> ing specific people's faces or their words. Nor was it about
> music or candles. It was simply, and most importantly, the
> presence of each person and the collective presence of lov-
> ing hearts, which was so soothing. I realize now that loving
> presence is Spirit. Within the presence is the individual
> person. The presence connects to everything. Presence is
> beyond time and space; it is vast and peaceful.*
> *Dying is not painful or even uncomfortable. Think-
> ing about dying is the beast. The body goes into a semi-*

comatose state as it shuts down. The consciousness or soul or spirit separates from the body and watches with curiosity, not with fear…but the mind…whew…the mind makes up stuff like crazy all the way through. For me, it sometimes felt like I was going crazy.

So, here's some advice: When in doubt, when the going gets tough, get out of your mind ASAP!

Toward the end, I was already going between realities. I discovered that my consciousness/soul/spirit was not affected by illness or medications. My body may have been dysfunctional, I may not have had the brain coherence to communicate, but my consciousness was always clear and perceiving everything on both sides of the veil. Perhaps this time of preparation is the gift of having a long illness as opposed to a sudden death. I have heard that there can be confusion with sudden death.

As I lay dying, I actually would dip into life on the other side, and then I'd be totally surprised when I awoke to discover I was still in bed and still alive!

For me, dying was something like when you lie down to go to sleep at night. There is a little bit of time where you might review the day before sleep and dreams take over. It is seamless, and the essence of "you" just keeps going.

The only mental tape I am still working to dismantle is feeling bad I was unable to beat cancer. I am learning that everything is perfect as it is; otherwise, it would be different.

Hmmm, right now I am starting to wonder if I have always had this underlying idea that there is something wrong with me, and blaming myself for not healing the illness is a distraction from the real issue. Okay, I get it.

That negative thought about myself used to run my life. So this is my chance…right where I am now…to correct that negative assumption about myself, once and for all. Dying was not a personal failure; it was the way to get to the real healing. Whew.

We all have another body made of less-dense matter, which reveals itself immediately once the physical body peels away. This lighter body has not been subjected to the ravages of the physical body or the physical world, so it is totally healthy and whole. My consciousness can easily modify this lighter body to make it appear younger, taller, thinner, etc. There's no need for makeup; you just create the look you want from the inside out!

You already know that our earthly physical bodies also reflect our thoughts and our consciousness. It just takes a lot longer for those things on the inside to be revealed in how we look and feel. The advice to think positive thoughts is literally true.

Here is one more piece to ponder. When more and more people are able to live a consistent flow of happy, loving thoughts and actions, they will heal, and the planet will heal as well. Healing yourselves is really simple. It is to be true to who you really are. Who you are is not a big mystery. The bottom line answer is L-O-V-E.

I love each of you. I am around when you call me in. Sometimes I just show up because I miss you and enjoy feeling your presence.

Hugs and kisses, and there are no misses!
Esther

"We all know we will go, and no one thinks they will."
    −Darla Singleton

___Darla's Message is a Poem

This Transmission from Darla Singleton came through
as a poem. She was thrown from her car in an accident
and died. Unbeknownst to me, she once earned her living by selling bubble bath. You will see the reference in
the poem. Her friend Tim, who requested the letter,
shared it at Darla's memorial service.

To All My Dear Friends

We all know we will go,
And no one thinks they will.
Oh my,
Who would have known,
My time would be,
To have been thrown,
Out the stage exit door,
From one world to the next.
What humor,
There is in the Mystery of it All.
I am feeling sad and mad and glad,
Not instantly free of all my,
Pains, sorrows and troubles,
But I am now in a balm of soft bubbles,
Dissolving all that,
And parts of me I need no more.
All that once comprised,
My existential rub,

Why Wait

All manner of things which,
Had gotten under my skin,
In this bath of love,
Are now permeated with filaments of light.
The dross will eventually,
Go down the tub,
As I let go,
And emerge again aglow.

As all of you,
Are doing so much for me in this now,
Know that I and legions of others,
Are here for you,
Whenever you call.
Love each other; drop the rest,
Create love bubble baths together,
Where nothing can fester.
You will thus contribute,
To the causes you cherish most,
Peace on Earth,
And connection with the Heavenly Host.

"I am sending all of you the biggest embrace, coupled with the wish that, like a fairy godmother with her magic wand, the gift of a greater awareness about life and death will expand your lives right now."
—Sara Marshall

___Sara is Delighted with Her New Experiences

Sara Marshall is exuberant about her after-death awareness and is excited to share about it. She tells us that we could all benefit by considering that death is an expanded state of being. She is now considering that what we call life is the more limited experience, and she would like to be our "fairy godmother" helping us to evolve.

> *Dear friends,*
>
> *I am in such an expanded state. I am thrilled and amazed to communicate with you. I am a "swoosh" of light, which has intelligence, awareness, love, and no boundaries. It gives me a giddy feeling to be part of the light of all life and still able to focus on the detail of this message.*
>
> *It is a bit awkward to be carrying on in such an excited way while I know that you and my family are experiencing the opposite since my departure. It makes me keenly aware that death is the expansive state and life in a body is the limited state of awareness.*
>
> *I am wondering if a new way to relate to the death of someone you love is to notice them holding open the veils, for you to glimpse the larger reality, and then bring that expansion back into daily life. That brings us closer, and it bridges our two realities. How exciting, and what*

a great way for those who pass over to serve the living. I never would have been able to make this observation if you had not asked to hear from me.

I don't like referring to the living or the dead because I want you all to know that I am very much living. Not with the same personality or the same form, but less form-bound and ever so much more aware. Everything is life, everything.

Thankfully, I have always had faith that everything works out and that love is the universal common denominator. This kind of faith goes way beyond any religion. The entire web of life is interconnected and is not random.

One of the things I am able to do from here is to serve as something of a "guardian angel," offering you and people who are on the Earth whom I don't even know, an infusion of universal faith.

Please, let all our friends know that I am excitedly exploring my new realm. I truly miss you and our conversations. I am sending all of you the biggest embrace coupled with the wish that, like a fairy godmother with her magic wand, the gift of greater awareness about life and death will expand your lives right now.

Sara

> *"It was like automatically zipping out of one skin, and into another, lighter one."*
> −Phil Jordan

Susan Introduces Her Friend Phil who is Very Relieved

My friend Phil Jordan was in his early fifties with beautiful white hair, which he wore pulled into a trademark ponytail and a short, neatly trimmed, white beard. He was soft-spoken, with intense blue eyes and an easy laugh that was more of a giggle.

We first met at an educational conference. He was a professional counselor, a gifted teacher and was also active in the governance of the organization. Phil inspired me to get more involved, too. And so, our collegial friendship began. When we eventually served together on the organization's board of directors, we would talk or email almost daily. Typical of Phil, most of our conversations were work-related.

Phil kept his private life mostly private. Now and then he would mention something personal. For example, he once let me know he was helping a young man in addiction recovery by providing him with a home, food, and guidance.

There were also hints of a deep sadness in Phil. Since he was devoted to supporting people to be the best they could be, it was difficult to observe how he didn't take as good care of himself as he did others.

The summer he died, Phil was at the airport on his way to our annual conference when his heart stopped. It was the 4th of July. The news of his passing was shocking, disappointing, and tragic on many levels.

My colleagues and I were aware he had some health issues, and many of us encouraged him to seek help.

As an added irony, I always valued his advice, which was to lighten the burdens in our hearts...advice he did not follow for himself.

Knowing our board would be gathering at the annual meeting only a few days after his death, and that his sudden exit would be difficult for many, I thought immediately of asking Carol if she would see if Phil might want to say something to us through her. Some of the board members were familiar with Carol's work, and I knew they'd welcome hearing from Phil via her.

She gave me a written Transmission from him that I took with me to the gathering. I immediately shared it with all of our colleagues and they took it on to others who loved him. The Transmission explained so much about Phil, and it gave comfort and helped ease feelings of shock and sadness for me and for everyone in our organization.

I had been especially upset imagining him dying alone in a public place, and I felt helpless that not one of us was there with him or had the chance to say any final words or thoughts to him. I was so glad he was receiving gentle, loving support in the "spirit" world. No small thing to know, he was able to feel this and to let it in.

Every morning at the conference, right after Phil's death, red cardinal birds came and perched on the balcony of my hotel room. We began to sense this was Phil telling us he was okay. We joked that Phil, who had been raised Catholic, was now elevated to Cardinal status.

It has been more than a decade since the Transmission from Phil helped so many of us. As the sky fills with fireworks every July 4th, I remember my friend, knowing he has found comfort, peace, relief, and love after death. Thank you, Carol, for providing the bridge between the veils.

    —Susan Sanborn

Dear Friends,

I am remarkably relieved and happy to be where I am. Carrying the cares of the world on my shoulders made me forget about humor, take myself too seriously and never smell the roses. I had no time for anything but pushing the boulder up the hill.

So it is a relief to be stripped of that heavy cloak. Right after the moment of death, the density of the physical world is shed. It was like automatically zipping out of one skin and into another, lighter one.

The Earth-bound me reacted to literally dropping dead from a heart attack with thoughts like: "This is serious. This is awful. Oh shit. What a mess. This is not good timing. I have not wrapped up my life neatly."

At the same time those thoughts I just mentioned were crossing my mind, my unzipped self was also chiming in. That part of me was saying, "God, this feels good. It's about time that I feel light and can enjoy myself, feel free and breathe again."

The guy you knew with the heavy heart is very sad to not be with you. Even though times have been more than trying for me in the last years, I am very loyal and do not take easily to giving up on anything I have committed to do. So, it bugs me to not have finished my work. From the heavy-heart persona, I feel very bad to leave you all holding my part of the bag. I did not like messes, and dropping dead in a public place is a disastrous mess.

The first step after my death was to be shown the stripped-naked truth about my life and death. The veils of illusion were lifted with incredible gentleness and not one ounce of judgment or punishment. The purpose is to then heal any underlying patterns, so they are never repeated.

What I had to see clearly in this loving light of non-judgmental truth is a part of me I had always tried to keep hidden from my friends. I do want to share this with you, so you have the full picture.

I was brought up that life is a sacred gift, and I considered myself to be very spiritual…but I found life to be very harsh, and I often wanted to die in order to escape. This line of thinking made me horrified at my cowardice and feeling guilty for my irreverence.

My heart took the brunt of my inner torment. I was aware that over the years, I had become a physical time bomb. All of you graciously gave me advice on how to be well, but I followed it only half-heartedly (pun intended). You could not have known how ambivalent I was about being healthier. I hope that you can find it in your hearts to forgive me for rejecting your caring efforts.

I am happy here and resolving all my inner conflicts with a great deal of loving support. Please know that I am truly grateful for your friendship over the years.

For now, I send all of you love, and I mean it. Please do all you can to lift whatever burdens you carry in your hearts while you are on Earth. Your lives will be so fulfilling, the Earth will be lighter, and then when you get to the other side, you will go to even greater heights of spiritual awareness.

"Imagine if you could experience that the air you are breathing is pure love...it truly is."
−Richard Potter

Richard Describes a State of Pure Love

This poetic and insightful love letter from Richard, a very spiritual young man, is to his fiancée, Laura. He perished in a tragic diving accident while on vacation with friends. Just as I am authoring this book with the help of my late brother, he suggests the idea of working from the other side with his girlfriend.

My dearest best friend and girlfriend Laura,

Imagine if you could truly experience the air you are breathing is pure love. It is. Imagine what a difference it would make to know that you are breathing in love, and how different life would be as that love permeates everything. Where I am, that's what it is like. There is no loneliness or sadness or harshness of any kind. There is no mental buzzing around and no wanting anything to be different from how it is. What a relief it is for me to be away from that kind of suffering and intensity.

You and I talked a lot about being in the present. In this love-filled environment, it is so natural to be in the present. There is no desire to escape to a past or to jump ahead to a future. This is the real deal, and I am so happy. I am at peace and so much better than I was.

Please cut me some slack while I make it sound so easy. I know it is hard to touch into this on the Earth plane. Experiencing the love that IS the air can happen more for you and everyone one Earth when you focus on the connections between all living things, rather than on the separation. Focus on what is right and beautiful, rather than what is frustrating or unpleasant.

And before you tell me, "Yes, good for you, and I am glad you are fine, but I am miserable," I would like to encourage you to notice some of the positive things happening now for you. Like, notice how many important questions about life, about spirit, about love and purpose are dancing around you for you to explore more deeply because of my death. Look how many old notions are crumbling within you so you can open to more expansion.

I would like to cheer you on to know there are big opportunities in front of you. We always loved the Buddhist teachings. Here is one we learned that you might practice now. Make a specific time each day to feel sad and mad. And then, when that allotted time is up, get on with the rest of the day in joy. Please stop torturing yourself. There is more to our story than a kick in the guts.

What if we can work together from our two different realities? And what if we can do that consciously, and what if you share with everyone that this kind of communication and ongoing collaboration is possible and waiting to happen more often?

I have a big grin right now imagining the possibilities.

I love you with all my heart. Everything is bigger than we imagine, and everything is connected. In that clear awareness of spirit, I am always with you.

Rick

P.S. I have enjoyed writing you this different kind of true love letter on your Valentine's Day. We don't have holidays here. Breathing love makes every day a holy day.

*"Ask yourselves, what would it take for each of you to
feel the truth of your worthiness while you are alive?"*
−Keith Atwood

Keith Transmits His Own Eulogy

Charles Summers had just lost his friend Keith Atwood
when he contacted me for a Transmission from Keith.
Charles then read this at Keith's memorial service.

Dear Friends and Family,

*My greatest challenge in life was to feel worthy and
lovable. I spent a lot of time and misspent energy chasing down validation and approval from everywhere but
right here inside me.*

*Where I am now with a bigger picture view, I can
also observe that when I was not feeling good about
myself, I had nothing positive to share with anyone else.
When I was able to connect with feeling worthy, there
was a generous overflow of kindness for, and connection
with, all of you.*

*Here is what I would like you to reflect upon today:
Only briefly bring to mind either the "good things" or the
"bad things" you remember about me. More important
to me is that you please take this time to realize in your
hearts how lovable you are. If you are in this gathering,
it means I hold you as worthy, lovable, and loved, regardless of the personality stuff of our relationships.*

*Ask yourselves, what would it take for each of you
to really feel the truth of your worthiness while you
are alive? God does not make mistakes. Everyone is
equally as valuable in the matrix of life; it is arrogant*

to exclude yourself.

If my experience is any small indication, when you know and feel you are lovable and loved, you will also have an automatic outpouring of good vibes for others. This adds up and makes a huge difference in the world.

It is easy for me to know all this now because most of my ego stuff has fallen away. Hopefully, these words and the feelings behind them can inspire you to drop any small, petty stuff right now. It may help you let go knowing all that drama does not matter in the end. Go and live your lives as you really intended. Earth is meant to be a paradise filled with abundance and joy.

Respectfully submitted from the other side…always here to help you have a smoother ride.

Keith

____Pearls of Wisdom

Good, honest and loyal friends are such a treasured presence in our lives. These friends continue to offer their support by sharing their insights for living our best lives and by asking us to continue to call upon them now as angel friends in another dimension of reality.

"…At the end of my life…It was simply, and most importantly, the presence of each person and the collective presence of loving hearts that was so soothing. I realize now that loving presence is Spirit." –Esther

"As all of you are doing so much for me in this now, know that I and legions of others are here for you whenever you call." –Darla

"One of the things I am able to do from here is to serve as something of a "guardian angel," offering you and people who are on the Earth whom I don't even know an infusion of universal faith." –Sara

"I send you all of my love, and I mean it. Please do all you can to lift whatever burdens you carry in your hearts while you are still on Earth. Your lives will be so fulfilling, the Earth will be lighter, and then when you get to the other side, you will go to even greater heights of spiritual awareness." –Phil

"What if we can work together from our two different realities? What if we can do this consciously, and what if you share with everyone that this kind of communication and ongoing collaboration are possible and waiting to happen more often." –Richard

"When you know you are lovable and loved, you will automatically have an outpouring of good vibes for others. This adds up and makes a huge difference in the world." –Keith

___Why Wait Meditation: Contacting Friends in Spirit

Following up on the idea of how to connect while awake with loved ones who are no longer with us, here is a simple practice with which you can quickly shift from concentrating the focus of your energy in your head to the heart. It is the human heart, which connects to the soul and offers the opportunity to access and perceive other dimensions of reality.

○ *Sit comfortably, and close your eyes.*

○ *Take three slow, deep breaths, inhaling and exhaling through the nose.*

○ *Imagine you can take a gentle elevator ride from your head down into your heart.*

○ *Once there, feel the experience of a lower center of gravity and how it is different from concentrating your energy in your head.*

○ *Continue focusing your attention on your physical heart, and imagine you can inhale and exhale through your heart.*

○ *Now bring your late friend or loved one fully into your awareness.*

○ *Feel the heart connection between the two of you.*

○ *Focusing on your heart and on their heart, ask them a clear question.*

○ *Receive the answer in your heart.*

○ *Take three deep breaths.*

○ *Review your experience.*

○ *Open your eyes, and maintain the heart focus as long as you are able.*

Chapter 6

Transmissions from Grandparents to Grandchildren

WHAT A WONDERFUL and mutually beneficial part of the design perfection of life it is to have grandparents and to be a grandparent. They are typically not as invested in, or distracted by, the struggles of our daily upbringing or their need to provide for us, which frees them from those responsibilities. Nor do we need to assert ourselves or rebel against them. Our presence gives grandparents a welcome dose of bright, young energy...and depending, of course, on who they are as people, grandparents tend to express their love to us more freely, forgive us more readily and spoil us more easily.

The clients in this chapter who have asked for the Transmissions from their grandparents have all been blessed with that special bond. These Transmissions are, not surprisingly, full of love, appreciation and warm, timely guidance for their now-adult grandchildren. The content is noticeably focused toward what they would like to pass on to their grandchildren and less on their personal self-reflections.

Not all of us have been blessed with knowing our grandparents, and not all grandparents are able to love unconditionally. However, the affection in these Transmissions is contagious and heart-warming. The clear, soulful words of wisdom from these grandparents are inspiring. Enjoy their love from the other side.

*"Sleep under the stars to know your place
in this world."*
–Dimitri Papadopoulos

Grandpa Dimitri Urges Connection to the Earth

Grandpa Dimitri's straight-from-the-heart teachings about our relationship to nature are relevant and true for everyone.

Dear grandson of mine…Dear Alex,

You honor me by asking to communicate; not many young people of your world seek a conversation with an old goat.

I am a product of the old country. We lived close to the Earth and close to God. We often thought the Earth and God were two different things, as if one was on the ground and the other in the heavens, but they are not two things. They are one in the same…all of it is God. All the wisdom I have to share with you is from my own life observing nature and people. You don't have to travel far to accumulate this knowledge. It is in front of everyone right where you are. The thing is to take the time to notice.

My life was about tradition and families living in the same part of the world more or less forever. We were all born, lived, and died in the same place. Now, that kind of life would give you claustrophobia. For us, it was a given and a comfort. Life will always bring changes, but in important ways, our routines, scenery, and families stayed pretty much the same. It helped with dealing with life. You might consider this boring.

In your life and in your world, with all the travel and opportunities that you have, please make sure to include the simple truths of life right in your backyard along with your big-world things.

Please pay attention to the Earth and cultivate something in the ground. You will find it humbling and inspiring. There is a very important relationship between you and the Earth and the plants and God when you participate.

Please take the time to watch the sunsets from twilight till dark. This will instruct you in the beauty of even the final phases in a day or in a lifetime. Also do the same with sunrises. Watch them from dark to daylight. You will feel comforted by being part of things in a new way.

Sleep outdoors under the stars to know your place in this world.

Find an activity you can do with your hands, which will allow you to participate in each separate season of the year. I am not referring to recreation, I wish for you the intimate participation in the cycles of the Earth and the seasons. Enjoy what this can teach you.

I admire your mother with all my heart and soul. She is a shining light and was always the apple of my eye. It is also true that I could never understand her. I thought it was excessive that she would always want more and more out of life. I was a parent like all parents who wanted my children to be happy, but I wanted them to keep the same values and traditions our family held for generations.

In my way of thinking, it is entirely possible to not understand your children and still love them. Certain things like that are a given.

Now, what am I doing and where am I? Not too much different, living simply. I have good friends. Some were my friends during my life who have also passed over. Some are new friends. I am being encouraged, in very loving ways, to be open to new things and to be a little frivolous. Sometimes I even put on a colored shirt!

I am learning to relax, and to be more allowing of life and of people and of things I don't agree with. In your language, I am learning to let go. Here that's quite easy; there are no awful or lasting consequences. Here you can watch alternative ways things can play out based on your attitudes, reactions, and choices. It's a lot like one of your interactive video games. (Ha, ha, do you like how up to date I am?) It is a fun way to learn.

I know that I still have a lot to learn and that sometime soon I will be back in your Earthly realms to put all this to the test. I just hope I get somewhere they have good land for a garden.

I remain your own grandfather...the old goat who always loves you.

P.S. Alex, tell your mother that there are no physical ailments here. I am fine; no aches and pains, and I go for long walks every day.

*"As craftsmen, we use materials of the Earth
and form them into new shapes and functions, which
they could not have done on their own."*

–Lars Johnson

Lars Reminds His Granddaughter About the Sacredness of Their Shared Profession

Lars Johnson was a craftsman, as is his granddaughter, Alissa. This Transmission has lovely wisdom about the nature of art. He even describes previous lifetimes when his soul and his current granddaughter's soul were artisans together in ancient civilizations.

My dear granddaughter, Alissa,

Though you credit me with giving you the inspiration to work with clay, you responded to all crafts since you were a little child. I am excited to tell you that we have been together in many lifetimes, and we have always shared a love of craftsmanship.

Sometimes the material we worked with was wood, sometimes stone. We have worked together on building cathedrals in Europe; we have crafted sailing vessels for Spain. Even longer ago, we carved statues of the gods and of some people who thought they were gods. These are connections we share, which I did not realize when I was alive, although I always felt a special affinity toward you.

We are blessed with knowing and practicing something very simple and profound. We use our hands to have a direct experience of sacred Creation. We use materials of the Earth and form them into new shapes and functions, which they could not have done on their own.

You asked for wisdom from me. Here are my most important suggestions based on what I can see troubles you, as it does many artists. You give yourself so much distress by wanting your art to only go to good people. Do not lose any sleep over where the things you create end up, or how others choose to make use of them. These considerations will limit your creativity and take you away from the purity of your gift.

Our ancient cathedrals remain special architectural beacons of light because their geometries are in Universal accord. This remains true regardless of the less than noble deeds of the people who have passed through the structures over the centuries.

Our ships were also more than pieces of wood fastened together with sweat. They were designed into forms, as were the cathedrals, which could inspire men to greater good. Those designs remain silently in higher service, even though they were too often used for wars and other lesser agendas.

Our statues, even the ones sculpted for arrogant people, were created with the proportions of the golden mean and stand as testimony to the higher truth of the design of the human figure.

Let go of your worries, and be true to your art. All enduring art follows the proportions of the Universe.

When you and I worked together, we never sought fame or fortune. We merely did our job. Sometimes that brought us wealth and the other rewards of mankind; other times it did not. We did not concern ourselves with the changing dispositions of man. We concentrated on the constant fulfillment of using our hands to amplify creation.

Another thing: I was never a talkative person. Why? For me, talk tended to muddle things rather than clarify them. My way of communicating was through my physical craft, or a firm handshake, a hug, a gesture or a glance. I relied on my kinesthetic sense to tell me the truth and to convey truth to others. Thankfully, I now have the advantage of being in a reality where there is not much chance that any form of communication can be distorted.

Before I get to sound like an old man repeating himself, I will end now. I am very content where I am, still maintaining the purest possible connection to God through creating form. Now, I am linking heaven to Earth; on the Earth I was always seeking connection to the heavens.

My love for you, like the hand-to-God connection, is eternal.

I am always your colleague and sometimes your grandfather!

P.S. If you are ever at a creative impasse relative to something you are working on, please call on me to assist you.

"Without realizing it, everyone who is alive on Earth is contained in something like an invisible bubble, which is a very, very thin 'film' created by everyone's thoughts and beliefs. It works like a one-way mirror, which people on Earth cannot see through."

–Grandma Costa

___Joseph's Grandmother is Happy to Tell What it's Really Like

Joseph Costa is a surgeon who has enough firsthand experience with people dying that he feels quite certain there is life beyond the cessation of the body. Though his grandmother passed away when he was a very young child, Joseph knows that his dad still struggles with whether or not the soul survives. Knowing that a Transmission from his grandmother could reassure his father in many ways, Joseph requested a Transmission from his deceased grandmother.

My dear son and handsome grandson,

Dying is not difficult, but leaving people you love is very hard. I am fine. I can see you and hear you and know how you are any time I choose to "look in." What is hard is that you cannot see me! I want to tell you that no one is ever dead. The body is dead, so the soul can no longer communicate through it. The soul is always "alive" and is aware of all of you, and so much more.

Without realizing it, everyone who is alive on Earth is contained in something like an invisible bubble, which is a very, very thin "film" created by everyone's thoughts and beliefs. It works like a one-way mirror, which people on Earth cannot see through. This is why the natural two-way communication between our realities is very difficult on your end. Most people cannot see beyond their "bubble." Neither could I, of course, during my life.

I would never have known this, considered this, thought it, or seen it during my life. I had my hunches about things sometimes, but I mostly kept those to myself...but now, I recognize those intuitive moments are when you break through the "bubble," and you can experience the two-way mirror between here and there and even beyond. Many people are afraid of this, but that's just another part of the limits of their "bubble."

I have to say, I am enjoying the chance to teach you people, who are smarter than I ever was, something new. (A mischievous, satisfied smile crosses her face.)

You ask if I am being treated well. Yes, and I am completely content. The second part of my answer is that every soul in this "other side" reality is treated well. If you have done awful things in your life, you are still met with love, and then you are helped to make an honest accounting and the necessary corrections. Even the difficult things to face about oneself are not a challenge to see or to let go of because it is done in the presence of the soul in an environment of pure love. Souls do not get defensive or insulted; souls can see what the personality did that was not okay. The accounting and correction process takes many forms and takes however long it requires; no one is counting.

You ask if I ever see your father and my handsome grandson's grandfather? This also works differently from what I expected. I am not with him, in the sense that he is not standing next to me, and we are not living together. How to explain this? It is beyond what I can understand, other than to say that in life when you think about someone, you can feel a connection to that person in your heart and mind. Well, if I focus my thoughts on someone I knew who is no longer alive, my "focused thought" seems to dial them up, and if they so choose, the person I knew literally shows up.

We interact for a while and then go our own ways. I know it sounds crazy, and I do not pretend to understand, no more than I can explain how a light bulb works. Maybe it just gives you an idea...but because his soul was part of my life, if I bring him fully into my awareness I can be with him any time I choose, and he does the same with me. Most of the time we are each busy with other things.

You wonder why I died so young. The answer is that age is not calculated by the soul, either. So, whenever the soul has finished what its sojourn on Earth was about, then it's time to let go of the body and move on. Naturally, people can do things to themselves making their lifespan shorter or longer. I had always prayed to be blessed to just close my eyes and die when it was my time, and I was prepared to accept my death whenever it would occur.

Well, that's not quite true. My one condition was that I not die and leave any young children. My prayers were granted. Something broke deep within my body, and I exited very gently with not a bit of pain or trauma. I was never afraid, and if I could even say so without meaning to hurt anyone's feelings, I was looking forward to "heaven," and I am happy.

Here is what I hope you can take from my telling you some of the new things I have learned. My wish is that you can now see there is nothing worth worrying about in life. Less worry equals more opportunities to poke holes in your limiting "bubble." So, live all your dreams! You are already good people. If a dream is meant to work out, it will. If not, get a new one! Please be happy, and be at peace. I look in on you often.

Your mother and Grandma Costa

P.S. In case you were wondering, I do not dress in black here!

*"What I want you to know is my soul was fine
and aware the entire time; it simply could no
longer rely on my body to express itself."*
−Molly Sharff

____Alzheimer's Robs the Body, but Not the Soul

Grandma Molly Sharff offers important and helpful information to know about the awareness of someone who suffered from and died from Alzheimer's disease.

My Dear Grandchildren,

I would like to say some things about Alzheimer's, which I experienced and could not communicate to you when I was ill. It does destroy brain function so that the soul has no ability to project the familiar personality anymore. Instead, you just get a jumble of biological misfirings with an occasional coherent communication.

What I wanted you to know is my soul was fine and aware the entire time; it simply could no longer rely on my physical body as the way to express itself. I had some occasional, quickly forgotten times of discomfort, but mostly I was out of there. It left you and the health care people interacting with a biological mechanism whose batteries had not run out, quite yet.

With all that said, the soul does know who is there and who is not present. Those heartfelt visits are felt and very precious. Obligatory visits are less gratifying, but the soul observes without any judgment.

Here is something else I'd like to mention to you about where I am now, which is very different and pleasant. Where you are, everyone has a name, and to get someone's attention, you use their name. Well, there are no names necessary here. There is instant recognition of another being…no need to have a name or even to call out to someone. Getting another person's attention is all accomplished through the mind. It is so efficient, and there is no such thing as miscommunication. You know this is a relief for me. I used to waste so much energy trying to get through to a certain person, also known as your grandfather; he was very difficult.

The question is, did I love him? The answer I offer you is that there are many kinds and degrees of love in an Earth life. I did love him, but not unconditionally. There is only unconditional love where I am now, which is entirely free of conflict and is peaceful.

Before I close, I want to add that I always felt a special soul connection with you. There was always unspoken love and understanding between us. This went beyond your age or mine. I am forever grateful for this, and its benefits are always mutual.

You can always call on me with your loving thoughts, and I will come to you. I am aware that you already know how to sense my presence.

So now get on with your own lives. Create your happiness and love.

Godspeed, Grandma Molly

____Pearls of Wisdom

Speaking from the love in their souls, these grandparents counsel us with a wealth of insights and sage advice for experiencing more lasting fulfillment in our lives.

"Please pay attention to the Earth and cultivate something in the ground. You will find it humbling and inspiring. There is a very important relationship between you and the Earth and the plants and God when you participate." –Grandpa Dimitri

"I would like to share some things about Alzheimer's, which I experienced and could not communicate when I was ill...The soul does know who is there and who is not present. Those heartfelt visits are felt and very precious. Obligatory visits are less gratifying, but the soul observes without judgment." –Grandma Molly

"Every soul in this 'other side' reality is treated well. If you have done awful things in your life, you are still met with love, and then you are helped to make an honest accounting and the necessary corrections. The accounting and corrections process takes many forms and takes however long it requires. No one is counting." –Grandma Costa

"We are blessed with knowing and practicing something very simple and profound. We use our hands [as artists] to have a direct experience of sacred Creation. We use materials from the Earth and form them into new shapes and functions, which they could not have done on their own." –Grandfather Lars

___Why Wait Meditation: Being in Nature

The living symphony of sounds, colors, textures, scents, shapes, energies, and the play of light outdoors in nature are designed to reset us to the natural rhythms of the Earth and our own DNA. The combination is like getting a massage for the soul. The reconnection is invigorating, soothing, healing, expansive, clarifying, beautiful, peaceful, and fun!

I recommend doing the following meditation, which Grandpa Dimitri has suggested in his Transmission, outdoors. I have also included an indoor version if you cannot be outside.

OUTDOORS

○ *If possible, stand or sit outside in silence at dusk, placing your bare feet on the Earth. Or walk in silence outdoors at dusk with bare feet as you do this meditation.*

○ *As you do this, take the time to silently watch a sunset from twilight till dark.*

○ *This will instruct you in the beauty of even the final phases of a day or in a lifetime.*

○ *Do the same with a sunrise.*

○ *Stand or sit outdoors in silence, placing your bare feet on the ground. Or, walk in silence outdoors with bare feet as you do this meditation.*

○ *Take the time to silently observe the sunrise from dark to daylight.*

○ *This will instruct you in the beauty of new beginnings emerging from the darkness.*

○ *You will feel comforted by being part of nature and the cycles of life in a new way.*

The brain assumes what you imagine is real, so the benefits of the following meditation are as valuable as being outside.

INDOORS

○ *Find a place to sit comfortably somewhere indoors where you will not be disturbed.*

○ *Close your eyes, and take three slow, deep breaths.*

○ *Bring to mind a favorite place in nature.*

○ *Make it really vivid in your experience by noticing all the special details of this place.*

○ *Imagine the colors, the textures, the temperature, the time of year, the scents, and how you feel in that environment of natural beauty.*

○ *Languish there for at least a minute, or for as long as you like.*

○ *Gently open your eyes.*

Chapter 7

Transmissions from Husbands and Wives

MANY SURVIVING SPOUSES report seeing their partner, feeling their partner's presence and/or having vivid dreams with meaningful conversations with them after they pass away. These happenings usually occur at night when people are more relaxed and less preoccupied with daily concerns.

Some wives have reported suddenly smelling the distinct scent of their deceased husbands' pipes or cigars when no one is smoking. Surviving husbands have likewise caught a whiff out of nowhere of their wives' favorite perfumes. Other uncanny experiences I have heard about often are turning on the car radio just as a couple's favorite song comes on the air...or having a book, which they both treasured, inexplicably fall off the bookcase. One client was at a nightclub in a foreign country on the anniversary of his spouse's passing when the singer randomly opened the evening set with the very song played at their wedding years ago.

To the skeptic, these are random events. For others, these are examples of how loved ones who are no longer alive are successfully getting their attention and finding ways to communicate meaningful messages.

As you read these Transmissions, you will discover that not every person on the other side has dismantled enough of their personal demons for their soul's wisdom to shine. Yet, all these people welcome the opportunity to communicate. They also offer reassurance, love, words of wisdom, and encouragement to their living partners... and to us.

*"Here I lie; my time was up for not paying attention.
I was driving along singing a song and not paying
attention. Story of an unnecessary end to my life."*
                        −Sean Michael

____Sean is Disappointed with Himself

Sean Michael's Transmission has a very different tone. He is furious that he died due to his own negligence, which continues with a very self-critical review of his life. Then as the communication to his ex-wife, Nancy, comes to end, he experiences a personal epiphany.

Dear Nancy,

This is about as unromantic as it gets. There I was driving alone, no other cars on the road, and I get killed. I could say, "Oh well, at least I did it my way." Given my theatrical career, I could make puns about stage exits or staged exits…but mostly I am pissed; pissed at myself for not paying attention. That could be the numero uno aggravation of my entire life of aggravations.

"Here I lie; my time was up for not paying attention. I was driving along singing a song and not paying attention. Story of an unnecessary end to my life.

I always wanted life to be fun, simple, a lark, an adventure without consequences. There was a time when I was a kid, when all there was to do in life was to get up, eat the breakfast made for me, go to school, come home to play, eat again, and go to bed for more of the same the next day; no responsibilities; no consequences; no paying attention. I always wanted life to be just like that kid feeling. As an adult, I just wanted to continue a

life of playing by being in theater, where I was paid for
playing in plays.

I was really blessed by having you in my life. I mean
that. You were always there to bolster me, to pick up the
pieces, to keep food on the table, to do the hard work
with raising the kids.

God knows I worked hard, and God knows my hard
work was fueled by anger and frustration rather than
pure creativity or joy.

I can see that part of getting killed was that I was
tired of trying to make life fun. I never did want to get
old, and I could never find the way to be an adult. To
me, being an adult meant no more fun, no more child
play. How's this:

"Here he lies, a great lad,
Never wanted to grow up
So, spent his life mad.
Had lots of talent,
And plenty of smarts
And charming to boot.
Because he wouldn't grow up,
He never earned much loot.
He just kept playing parts,
Offering empty promises
And breaking people's hearts."

OMG, something profound just happened. All of a sudden this diatribe of mine has no fuel. Peace has come
over me. I have never felt like this…ever. Everything is
suddenly spacious and vast and calm. There is no more

hype. This is very new.

Now I can also see you all feeling so bad and sad. I had not noticed till right now. I am really sorry. I guess it has always been all about me. I am so sorry. Maybe this is what it took for me to see.

Later, Sean

> *"I would love it if you could learn to recognize*
> *the sensations in your body that occur when*
> *I am contacting you. With practice and*
> *awareness, you will know it is me."*
> −Martha Harrold

Martha Describes Her Sudden
Death and Reassures Her Husband

Martha Harrold died in an automobile accident. Hers is a very clear and reassuring account of how the soul instantaneously separates from the body and can calmly observe the carnage. She is also eager for her husband, Alan, to learn to recognize the presence of her spirit.

My dear Alan,

I am so happy to be communicating with you. I can always see you, and sometimes I even talk with you, though I am aware you don't consciously hear me. However, I observe that you always react, even though you don't know what's going on.

I was totally caught by surprise by my death, hit by an oncoming car. I had just one split second of a thought, "Oh no," ...and then I was expecting to feel hurt or panic or pain, but none of that happened.

I was immediately watching the whole thing, sparing me of any pain. I was actually feeling calm and peaceful. I felt surrounded by love, a kind of love that makes you feel calm and not alone or worried or upset. This love was even stronger than what you can feel as a child in your mother's arms.

So, I watched and listened to it all. The carnage was

ugly. I had one more brief thought at the time which was, "Oh God, what about you?" I saw you and put my arms around you. I know you felt me without knowing it because in that moment you thought about me. You had no idea I was there, and I had no idea what had really happened to me yet, either.

Until that experience, I had not realized these subtle levels of communication existed. Now, I can see that everyone is always bombarded by thoughts from people who are alive and people who are not, and that people on both sides are reacting to each other all the time without realizing it.

I would love it if you could learn to recognize the sensations in your body, which occur when I am contacting you. With practice and awareness, you will know it is me, and maybe someday you might even be able to understand what I am "saying." Trust me, my messages are not complicated.

The main thing I am excited about is that I am alive, just not in the exact reality or in the same way you are. I can now tell you there is no reason to hold back in life or to not do things you really want to experience for fear you might die. No one dies; the body does.

I love you always and thank you for just being open. All my love, Martha

*"...Here, I have to pay attention to everything,
because everything I think or say plays out
right in front of me."*
–Andrew Silber

____Andrew Redefines Heaven and Hell

Andrew Silber has a lot to say about the concepts of heaven and hell, and continues with more about the importance of paying attention both in life and afterwards. His tone toward his wife, Elaine, is supportive and affirming, and the keen observations he makes about life are valuable for everyone.

My dear Elaine,

I am not in heaven or hell. Both of those are words and concepts, which people use and some believe. What is more accurate is that where I am, every thought, every attitude and every belief plays itself out in front of you like a movie. If I am mad, then the whole scene where I am, including clouds and nasty weather, gets ugly as a reflection of my anger. If I am happy and feeling terrific, the colors are so bright, the birds are singing, and everything I gaze at looks beautiful. I get to see immediately how I "color" my world and my worldview by my own stuff. Cool, huh? So, this is how I create my "heaven" or my "hell."

Now, you are very smart, so you've already figured out that this is exactly how it works in life, too. Only, it is so much less obvious when you are "alive on Earth." I put those words in quotes because I am definitely very much alive. It is as if I am on a different radio bandwidth than you are. It is hard for you to pick up on me, but I can see you and even pick up on your thoughts. I can hang out near you just by thinking that's what I'd like to do. Can you tell when I check in on you?

Anyway, I do not mean to be flippant, just light-hearted. I have really come to realize that in my life I was sarcastic a lot and said things I did not always mean. I did not pay attention to what I said and how I said it. Not just to you, but this was true in general... but here, as I already told you, I have to pay attention to EVERYTHING because what I think or say plays out right in front of me. This is helping me learn how to pay attention and how to choose what I do and do not want to have show up. I am getting better at this. Okay, slowly I am learning to watch my mouth.

At first when I died, I was so mad. It is one thing to be feeling really down in life and say, "Maybe I'd be better off dead," and it is another thing when that comes true because I did not really mean it. It all happened so fast. Oh, I can tell you, I am going to pay attention in my next life. I am also going to say only what I mean, be true to myself and be a better person for it. I hope this makes you smile.

I can tell you to please stop beating up on yourself for things you said or did not say during our time together. I am fine. Don't waste time and energy in life wondering "what if?"...that is just another word trick to stall and to convince yourself to not get on with your life. I want you to live a good life. There are no mistakes. Where you are in your life, who you are with and what you are doing is not a mistake. Please try at least to see it that way. I want you to be happy. I can see that you have a very long life ahead of you. You know the joke: If you live long enough, you get old.

One more point. Everyone in the world would be happier if they made certain to tell the people they love… "I love you"… every day, and to not let things simmer or be stuffed.

I would like you to say "Hi" from me to the few of my friends who can handle this kind of message from the "beyond." You know the ones I mean. One more time, please pay attention to what makes you happy. I have enjoyed "talking" with you.

I love you every day, Andrew

*"I have learned that there is a higher plan,
and that sometimes, a healing does not mean
you get everything you want."*
−Stuart Cameron

____Julia Introduces Her Husband, Stuart, Who Honors Her with a Heartfelt Tribute

When I lost my husband, in January 2006, it was hardly a shock, or a surprise. He had been ill with cancer for several years, but he had continued to work, to travel and to lecture to his students almost without a break. It was only in November of 2005 that we realized that the cancer had gotten to the point where he could no longer do this. Then there was a change of venue, involving hospitals and eventually the local hospice, where he stayed for three weeks before deciding that he wanted to die at home, surrounded by those he loved, which was how we came to January 30. He died early in the morning.

From that moment onward, I coped because of course I had to−with the help and support of my two daughters, my husband's two daughters, and all our friends. I continued to travel to America, France, and Spain where the two of us had been accustomed to going annually...but inside, I was falling apart: I had not come to terms with the loss in any way at all−my husband was an extraordinary man, "larger than life," and just to think about him and our life together turned me into a weeping wreck. Five years on, during my visit to the States to see my daughters, I was still absolutely numb with grief until one of my daughters suggested that talking to Carol might be a good idea.

I was skeptical and had never believed that anyone could communicate with those who had "passed over."

But I sent Carol an email outlining the barest minimum of information and went to visit her a week later. I was not expecting anything...but I left, an hour later, carrying the Transmission, as she called it, which she had written as a result of her thinking about my husband.

The Transmission was an extraordinary document, covering two pages of paper that sounded exactly as if he had written it. She even referred to him by his nickname, which I had not told her. Some of the things he wrote about made the hair on my arms stand up; these were details of his life, which he had shared with me, and I don't think with anyone else. His words of comfort for me were indescribable. For the next few weeks, I read and reread these pages. I shared them with my daughters and his daughters, and now I believe I have accepted that he may be gone in a physical sense, but that he is still with me in many, many ways, all of them comforting and real.

–Julia Cameron

My dear Julia,

Once in a very great while there is a great love. You will always be that for me. Thinking about you always evokes in me the poet, the romantic, and the man of high ideals. You rekindled in my soul the realization that true love is possible.

It was never my conscious intention to die and leave you. May I please affirm that before you, no matter how it may have appeared on the outside, I had never experienced true love. In fact, I long ago put away the idea that it was even a real possibility in life. Being the romantic, this had always been a painful disappointment deep within me. *My life was good enough before we met, and I felt I had no right to complain.*

Being with you and sharing our love healed a deep place in me, which allowed me to feel "watered" deep in my soul. I fervently wish the outcome of my healing could have been to stay alive and enjoy so much more with you. I have learned that there is a higher plan and that sometimes, a healing does not mean you get everything you want.

I am "writing" this letter as a tribute to you. If I could, I would compose a sonnet. If we had known that our love would heal me, but not allow us to spend long-lived lives together, would I have married you anyway? If the roles had been reversed and you had left first, would I have married you anyway? I am saying a resounding YES on my part. I would never miss this opportunity to be with you, no matter how long or how short. If I were the one planning it all out, there would only be one caveat…that you would suffer less.

Here is what I am being told by my mentors here to offer you. The loss of a beloved is heartache seemingly beyond all measure…and there are only two responses to this situation, both of which are a choice. One response leads to a lifelong constriction of the heart, accompanied by physical decline, less life force, no pleasure, and a loss of faith.

Or, along with the grief, it can be the door to great expansion and personal growth. When the heart is "broken open," beyond the pain is more love, more gratitude, new and renewed awareness of how precious everyone and everything in life truly is. Grief is love. Sadness is love. Anger is love. Joy is love. Everything is actually love. My greatest wish is that you continue to find meaning, beauty, and joy in your life.

I hope you will continue to count your blessings every day. If it would be helpful when you are wondering how to proceed, you might say to yourself, "What would I want for you?" or "What would I want you to do?" No one who has died would ever want anyone they loved who is still alive on the Earth to shut down and to stop living because we are not physically there. It is also a misstatement of the whole truth to say, "until death do us part," because I am here to tell you there is no death… there is no apart, except in the physical body. My mind, my heart, my spirit and even some of the cells of my body continue to be a part of you.

It is self-punishment to reject life. You and I are special to each other eternally. Make me your guardian angel. Live an even fuller life; develop your talents, help other people, smell the flowers, see the beauty.

I don't know how else to make my point clear. The highest act of love for me and the highest act of love toward yourself is to open again to the miracle of life.

That great and true love of ours is meant to restore in you now…as it has in me…the indescribable comfort of knowing this kind of love is real and that we have experienced it and know it to be true. It is not about whether it was taken away. It is about what is given, which can never be taken away.

Smell the roses, gaze at the stars, listen to the birds, touch a child's hand, enjoy the seasons, revel in the feel of clean sheets and a soft quilt…life is beautiful.

*I am restored to total health. I toast you. Please lift
your glass and also toast how precious life is. The highest
form of devotion is to live a full and joyous life.
Always I am yours.*

____Pearls of Wisdom

Here are some more loving pearls from husbands to
their wives and vice versa. Hopefully, if you have lost a
spouse, a lover, or anyone you have loved, they have
shown up in your dreams to offer comfort and even
guidance. More about that opportunity follows these
quotes.

*"I would love it if you could learn to recognize the sensations in
your body that occur when I am contacting you. With practice
and awareness you will know it is me, and maybe someday you
might even be able to understand what I am 'saying.'"* –Martha

*"I was really blessed by having you in my life. I mean that. You
were always there to bolster me, to pick up the pieces, to keep
food on the table, to do the hard work with raising the kids.
Now I can see you all feeling so bad and sad. I had not noticed
till right now. I am really sorry. I guess it has always been about
me. I am so sorry. Maybe this [my death] is what it took for me
to see."* –Sean

*"I can tell you to please stop beating up on yourself for things
you said or did not say during our time together. I am fine. Don't*

waste time and energy in life wondering "what if?"…that's just another word trick to stall and to convince yourself to not get on with your life. I want you to have a good life." –Andrew

"When the heart is broken open, beyond the pain is more love, more gratitude, new and renewed awareness of how precious everyone and everything in life truly is. Grief is love. Sadness is love. Anger is love. Joy is love. Actually, everything is love. My greatest wish is that you continue to find meaning, joy, and beauty in your life." –Stuart

____Why Wait Meditation: Asking to Dream about Them

It is such a comforting experience when someone we have lost appears in a dream. One year after my brother died, I had a dream in which he came to me with a bouquet of flowers right before my birthday. In the dream I was so surprised and blurted out, "What are you doing here? I thought you were dead." To that he replied, "I am only dead in the reality you are in."

Here are some ways to set the stage for inviting that special loved one to appear in your dreams. Be open to recognizing that dream messages come in many forms, including but not limited to: conversations, symbols, music, book titles, and even familiar scents.

The more you relax about this and the more you practice these steps, the easier and more rewarding it will be. Please make this a fun bedtime exercise (it is not a test) and be curious what you might dream. Keep in mind the reason we have access to other dimensions of reality in the dream state is precisely because we are in a different brain wave pattern, deeply relaxed and disconnected from daily preoccupations.

The first step is getting enough natural sleep. We dream in approximately ninety-minute intervals, and the longer we are asleep, the longer each dream period lasts. The longer a dream lasts, the more likely we can recall it. For example, scientists report that dream length may start at ten minutes early in the night, while by the time we are sleeping eight hours, a single dream can last up to 45 minutes.

○ *Set your intention at night in two ways.*

○ *First, just before you turn off the lights, write down your intent that you will have clear dream communication with a specific person on the other side, and you will remember your dreams.*

○ *Second, as you are drifting off to sleep, bring awareness of that special person into your heart.*

○ *Holding them in your heart, tell them you are open to receive them in your dreams and ask them to please appear in them tonight if they are able.*

○ *Close your eyes and fall asleep.*

○ *When you awaken, do not shift your body position.*

○ *As you lie there not quite fully awake, focus awareness in your heart and ask your heart, "What was I just dreaming?"*

○ *Stay in your heart, feel into it, and enjoy the dream segments and/or sensations you are able to retrieve.*

Chapter 8

_Transmissions from Two Murder Victims

THE UNTHINKABLE SHOCK and loss of a loved one who is murdered is impossible to imagine. A life has been cut down without any notice. There is no time for good- byes, nowhere to get answers, and survivors are challenged to examine their core beliefs in order to come to peace and move forward in their lives or become another victim of the crime. Another part of this worst nightmare for the surviving relatives and friends is imagining what fear and pain the person must have endured as they were dying.

As always, I never know what the soul who has passed will choose to share. Souls have an uncanny ability to offer exactly what the survivors need to know to be able to move on. Those on the other side are very clear that giving up on one's life, or being consumed with rage and revenge, only gives the perpetrator more power.

Both of these murder victims were women. In the first case, and unbeknownst to me, the surviving mother had not been able to engage with her own life since the crime. The Transmissions from her daughter are so clearly focused on helping her mother. The second family was still unsure what had actually happened. They needed to know more details, to know there was nothing they could have done differently, and to somehow let go of being consumed with rage.

Thankfully, these Transmissions helped set minds at ease and hearts on the path to deeper healing. There are two separate Transmissions from each of these murder victims. They share remarkable self-awareness, love for their family members, and wisdom about life and death for us to apply to our lives. Please note that though these victims reveal they are not suffering and are now at peace, this information in no way is meant to condone acts of violence.

"It is fine to want justice in order to remove sick and hateful people from the world. But I do not want you to be so obsessed that you don't have a life. If you continue like this, there will be two unnecessary deaths...mine and yours."

–Julie Stoughton

___Julie Wants Her Mother to Get a Life

Julie was murdered by a group of strangers in a senseless, random act of violence when she was studying abroad. In her Transmission, she is focused above all on wanting to help her mother. You will note that this young woman is not at all wallowing in the circumstances of her death, nor is she taking on the stance of victim.

Dear Mom,

You are driving yourself crazy and ruining your life over this, and that is not okay. Not with me, and not with God. I have been trying to tell you this for a long time, and I am so happy my message is finally reaching you. Even before I was killed, you were always worrying about everything and everyone and taking care of everyone, except yourself. This behavior of yours is frustrating for me to watch, but it has to be worse for you to live your life like that. There is nothing that says you cannot enjoy your life and still work on the crime.

It is fine to want justice in order to remove from the world sick and hateful people, but I do not want you to be so obsessed that you don't have a life. If you continue like this, there will be two unnecessary deaths...mine and yours.

I want you to heal and then to talk about your experience. There are others who need to know how to recover from such a loss. You can inspire them and offer guidance. With my communication, you have even a bigger picture perspective to offer others who are suffering from the loss of murdered loved ones.

In the big picture, it is all life. Life and death are life. No one dies, except to shed the physical body...and, by the way, while I am on that subject, I wish you would treat your body better. Keep in mind that it's the only one you have for getting around on Earth, and it can tell you lots of things you need to know, when you pay attention.

Mom, remember the game of hiding things and then telling someone that they are getting warmer or colder, depending on whether they are nearer or farther from whatever has been hidden? Well, I can work with you like that by helping to reinforce the feelings you have in your body when you are on the right track in your investigations of this crime. This will let you know you are getting warmer. When you are onto something, your usual feeling in the gut will be superstrong, so you can't ignore it. When it is a false lead, there will be no gut feeling at all. It's a good experiment, which you can practice just by calling me in to help, and then by asking your questions out loud. If you are ever in the presence of the criminals, I will make sure your body is screaming at you.

I know what I am about to say will sound impossible to you, but it is true that during the awful acts, which led to my death, I did not feel much pain at all. I definitely felt that time was frozen, and I had that sinking, "Oh shit, I cannot believe this is happening to me" feeling of terror when they grabbed me. After that I was numb… in my emotions and in my body. If I wasn't unconscious, I was for sure out of my body looking down at the scene. I could see what they were doing to me and could not feel a thing. I was definitely thinking as I was watching, "Oh God, what they are doing to my body?"

It is an odd thing, now that I still have a body, and I look like I always did…except that I don't have even a microscopic blemish on my skin anywhere. You know how obsessed I could get with little things like that!

When I first arrived here, I was met and given the most extraordinary loving care. I was told what happened because even that was blocked out by my overall numbness during the crime. I was taken to a place to recuperate from the trauma. It was like being bathed in love 24/7; no worries; no pain; no loneliness; no fear; no tension; nothing but comfort and gentleness.

Here is the most important thing I have to say to you. No one has to die to be free of worrying. No one has to die to feel real love. You do have to let in the support and the love. You do have to notice that both love and support can be found everywhere if you are paying attention.

There was nothing you could have done differently in relation to me. You yourself always said that when your number's up, your number's up…they find you if it is your time. Please know that even when you are tormenting yourself about how, if only, we had lived somewhere else…it was my time, and no matter where in the world we might have been living, something like this would have happened anyway.

I will be learning and understanding more about why me and why this way and how to use this experience for the better. I will let you know. Please promise you will do the same thing...using this difficult experience for the better...in your life now.

I love you and I always will.

"Please concentrate on what you and I shared,
not on what you don't have."
—Julie Stoughton

____Julie's Second Message to Her Mother

Once again, Julie is strongly urging her mother to get on with her life and to use the tragedy to help others. There is a valuable insight here about the waste of time and energy that can happen in anyone's life if they adopt the identity of "victim."

Dear Mom,

You know that our family members are not the most patient people in the world, so please take what I have to say next with a lot of love and many grains of salt.

I want to tell you to get your butt in gear. Find something that interests you, in which you can really get involved. Do something that grabs your full attention and makes you feel good at the end of the day because you've done something that benefits others.

The worst thing is to live your life focused on your own misery and loss. It wears you down and paralyzes you, as you have noticed. Living in a state of constant victimhood takes you away from any form of pleasure and fulfillment, not to mention that you are robbing yourself (another crime) of that little three-letter word, J-O-Y. All this self-torment does no one any good, and it certainly does not bother my killers.

You might wonder why I am so insistent with wanting you to turn your life around. The first reason is that I love you and want you to live well. Then there is also the fact that when you think about me, and you do a lot, it is as if you are calling me, and I feel the tug, along with your sadness and despair.

It is never a good reason to do something because someone else wants you to…but in this case, would you please consider enjoying your life and respecting the gift that it is…for my sake. Might it relight your passion for life if you see yourself living for both of us?

When you think of me, please concentrate on what we shared, not on what you do not have. The truth is, I am always around you and can help give you comfort…if you let me. Just like when I was alive and physically with you, I could only help you when you let me.

Anyway, I am truly fine. It does not matter to me anymore whether the crime is solved. Everyone "gets theirs" eventually in one way or another. You can trust this law of the Universe.

I continue to be learning so much about how life really works…and most exciting is that I have made enough progress so that I am now able to help people on this side, who have died traumatically, to make peace with and to understand their situation.

Please remember there are so many children alive on the Earth who need a mother or a mother figure. Maybe you would like to do the same kind of work I am doing, on your side of the fence.

I love you always, Julie

"Maybe just one woman will listen to the warning signs better than I was able, and save her life. It is so sad that it was more important for me to please him than to live."
—Emily Morrison

———Anne Introduces Her Sister Emily who Paid with Her Life

Carol,

Thank you for validating what we "knew in our hearts"…my sister Emily died of foul play.

The day before my sister and best friend died, I spent fifteen minutes chatting with her on the beach telling her what I thought of this man she had brought with her on our vacation together. I had never experienced a man with such negative energy. Talking with her about him, these words spontaneously flew out of my mouth: "Em, this man will chew you up and spit you out."

She looked into my eyes and we shared a "moment" that only sisters who are so close can do. It was a soul-to-soul connection unlike anything I have ever experienced. In that powerful, silent exchange I knew that she knew that what I was saying was the truth. Twenty hours later, she was dead.

I am still in great shock and find myself uncontrollably weeping. What really happened here? Someone please wake me up from this nightmare. We had rented a lovely house on a secluded beach, and we were all gathered there to celebrate Emmy's birthday. Who would ever believe she would instead be cremated on her birthday?

Carol, you do so many readings, so you may not

recall the Soul Reading you did for Emily a few years ago, so I am going to remind you because it was all brought back to me in a very helpful way when she died.

Two years ago, Emily and I came to the session together and decided to listen in on each other's Soul Readings. Since we were so close and enjoyed many of the same things growing up together, I assumed the content of our Soul Readings would be alike. I remember saying while Emily went to the restroom, "Well, I'll bet her reading will be similar to mine." I'll never forget the expression on your face as you said to me with eyebrows raised, "The two of you have very different soul histories and current learning lessons."

Briefly, you told Emily that the main course correction for her in this life is to discover the meaning of true love and to, therefore, not repeat the pattern of being fooled and seduced by abusive men with their promise of fame, fortune, or social status. Emily needed to learn that real love has nothing to do with these.

In that session, Carol, you went on to alert Emily to the many "red flags" in her pattern of current relationships with men. You urged Emily to recognize and pay attention to the numerous warnings that she was being used and manipulated by men because these behaviors are not about love. You told her to take action. Listening to all this, Emily got fidgety and blurted out, "Oh my God!" I looked at my sister rather shocked, like WHAT?!

Emily said that the kind of man Carol described was just exactly like the man she had just divorced, and that though there were always lots of men interested in her, she usually went for those who seduced her, promising great things, and sooner or later, they turned out to be cruel.

Whoa. I had not seen this coming. Suddenly, the

wheels were turning in my head, and I saw Emily's pattern with men. I had not put this together before. My sister was a magnet for men. We would walk into a nightclub or even a restaurant and heads would turn. She would be wooed and swept off her feet quickly, and there was always a drink in front of her. I was shy, and I began to notice that we attracted radically different types of men. She attracted the "bad boys." She went with men who I would avoid like The Plague.

When my sister died, Carol Mann was the first person I called after notifying the rest of our family. Carol promised to do the Transmission right away. She mentioned Emily's soul was still hovering over the area, so after we hung up the phone, the kids and I walked down the beach to where I "felt" she died. My young son spontaneously wrote a huge "We love you, Emily" in the sand. My daughter, who was barely four at the time, was gently tossing flower petals in the water at my side. I stood ankle-deep in the warm ocean and totally felt my sister's presence.

Out of nowhere, a white bird circled over the sea right there in front of me. It truly appeared out of nowhere...I never saw it fly in. I said out loud with tears pouring down my cheeks, "Go now, Emily. Go. You are free. Go home. Go to the light. Be free." The bird circled another time or two, and once again, I bid her my final farewell and that bird disappeared in the sky just as quickly as it had appeared. The bird did not fly away; it simply vanished.

Something Emily said in her Transmission through you on the day she died has stuck with me, and has been the crux of allowing my other sisters and me to accept and even understand what happened. In the Transmission, my sister said, "The big thing here is no blame. Everyone played their part perfectly. Just learn from it."

On reflection and talking with my other sisters, I realize now that everyone did play their parts perfectly. We took this trip to celebrate Emily's 50th birthday. We wanted all of my sisters to be there and her daughters, our spouses, and anyone else who could join in. It was going to be great...but it turned out that of my five sisters and their families, only my oldest sister and her husband, Bruce, my kids and I could go.

In the big picture, just like in a play, certain characters were needed and selected. Those of us there were the chosen ones, and we did play our parts perfectly. Had many others been along, no doubt things would have been crazier and more difficult.

Because of the big age difference, my oldest sister, Karen, did not really know Emily very well, but she was the perfect person to be there to pick up the pieces. Karen held me together when my world fell apart. She handled the necessary details in cremating and bringing Emily's remains home, and her husband Bruce was another "rock."

Karen and I feared the perpetrator might come back after us in the night because he knew that we knew what he had done. Having my sister's burly husband present was critical. As for my kids, well, unfortunately, they were there to witness extreme trauma, but they coped, and I trust that experience may help them down the road someday.

Recently, my dad called me and told me I was carrying the weight of responsibility for Emily's death. He continued emphasizing how I must let go of that because it was not my fault. I realized there was truth to his comment. It's taken a while to process, but on that beach when she and I had that unique soul-to-soul connection and I knew she knew that what I said about the man was truth, well, what else could I have done? I told her. She understood. Yet, she did not have the courage, the balls, or whatever you call it to stand up to him and tell him it was over.

She was an adult, with the information I had given her the day before. Actually, I warned her twice about this guy who, like her abusive recent ex-husband, was luring her with extravagant gifts, promises of travel, and wealth. I warned her she was falling for the same awful kind of person again, and she had the benefit of the information of her Soul Reading a couple of years ago.

I have come to terms with the fact that I really did do what I was supposed to do by warning her, and by seeing that she had the information. She brought him on this trip, and it was not my job to ask him to leave. He was her significant other, not mine. Of course had I known he was going to end her life, I would have done something, but who would ever have thought that?

And then all of a sudden, all that you said in her Soul Reading made incredible sense. This lifetime was given to her as the opportunity to grow, to understand and to evolve away from being a victim. The stage was set. Red flags had been flying throughout her life, but she did not "see" them. She was playing the part perfectly of being helpless.

Though she had a choice, right up until the point where she entered the water with him, Emily did not act on the opportunity she had to get out of the situation.

I cannot even imagine what we would all be going through without the insight into the "bigger" picture. The heartache and grief would be too much to endure. What we know in our hearts, and from the Transmissions and from processing all this together, is permitting us to find closure and acceptance of a dreadful tragedy.

My sisters and I can't thank you enough for "listening" to Emily, for getting up in the middle of the night to receive her messages to us. Those messages revealed way more about her than we could have ever known. They filled in the missing gaps and pieces of the puzzle...and I believe her when she said not to worry about her perpetrator, as his karma will take care of him.

I can only hope that by telling this story, some woman or women will find the courage to stand up, take no more and get help right away. Otherwise, the victim pattern will sadly continue until they take action.

—Anne Morrison

Dear Anne,

You warned me that he was pushing the limits, yet I continued to stay with him. I feared he would reject me if I did not go along with him, and then I'd have another failed relationship. I paid with my life for copping to my fears and not having the courage to say "no" to him. It is pathetic to think that I placed so little value on my life. It is so sad that it was more important to please him than to live.

This was not the first time he pushed me. He had a terrible temper. He likes weak women, women who are in distress so he can step in as the hero, the protector, the "I'll make it right for you; you can count on me" type. He knows what to say to each potential victim, and then poof, they are having an affair in which he is taking emotional and often financial advantage of the vulnerable woman.

He knows exactly whom he can move in on, and he knows when his prey is perversely ready to be taken.

Oh my God, this is so much to grasp. I have not yet left the scene of the crime; I am hovering. My angels are with me. They are working on my heart, not to revive it, but to make sure that I do not blame myself. They are here to ensure that I don't add another huge ding to my lack of self-esteem. The angels are pouring love into me; I can feel it as it takes away all the pain. I am very peaceful and loved.

At the same time, everything is running through my mind. Every thing. Please tell everyone how much I love each one of them. None of you are at fault. Everyone played their part perfectly. We can all learn something from this. My goodness! What a way for me to learn to value my life. You know, he could have saved me, and he didn't. He got scared and felt a thrill at the chance to kill me. He is sick.

At last, I can see that trying to earn someone's love is ridiculous. They either love you or they don't...and I also get it that if I am not occupying myself with trying to get a man's love, I will be able to see more clearly who they truly are. I won't be blinded by my insecurities. Therefore, I will be able to make better choices. I get it now.

Please love one another. Love yourselves. I love you. I feel loved right now in a way that I have never known.

P.S. Revenge is not the path for you in relation to this crime and my death. Instead, please go out and talk to weak, hurting women in abusive relationships.

Encourage them to put pride aside and to get help. Tell them also to follow the advice of the counselor, no matter what. Maybe just one woman will listen to the warning signs better than I was able, and it will save her life.

*"Look up the word 'sociopath.' He knew how to
provide everything I wanted and had ever dreamed
of...for a while...till he got me totally in his control."*
—Emily Morrison

Emily's Second Message: She Sees Why She Picked Cruel Men

My dear sisters,

Why did I get involved with mean men? Because I had low self-esteem when it came to intimate relationships with men. Where I am now, I have a lot more insight as to how that came about. Because I realize you are aware that being sexually abused as a child can trigger future abusive relationships, I do want to clear that up and say that I was not abused as a child. There is no need to torment each other further wondering if there is a secret perpetrator in the family.

In my case, there were reasons from previous lifetimes, which needed to be addressed and healed in this lifetime. Many of you called me on my self-destructive pattern with men. Others of you tried to get me to listen, to wake up. But I did not listen to anyone.

I preferred to believe lies and excuses, and to overlook the obvious signs that this person was potentially violent. I did not want to pay attention to the now-obvious red flags. I liked to think that I was different, even if I knew the awful past history of this person. Given my attitude, I was a perfect setup. Look up the word 'sociopath.' He knew how to provide everything I wanted and had ever dreamed of...for a while...till he got me totally in his control.

By then, I did not want to believe my ears and eyes, because I didn't want the dream to end. My fantasy knight had gaping holes in his armor, and I refused to see them. He had me so confused I wasn't even sure if the bad things were my fault or his.

So that night when we were alone, I started asking him some probing questions about inconsistencies in his stories, and he got very agitated. He threatened me with, "Don't ever question me!" He got physically rough, too. He pushed me and held me down to show off his dominance…letting me know I should beware of the person I was messing with. And then we had sex, which was more confusing, but he said he loved me, even though it did feel like rape, which sealed the deal of who was in charge.

The next day we went for a long walk and a swim, and I was scared, but hoping everything would be fine. He was silent as we walked, and you know how much I hated the silent treatment from anyone. And then we went into the water. I was still hoping it would change. I commented about the silence, which just set him off.

We were deep in the water, and there were some huge waves that day. I was tired from hardly sleeping the night before, and I couldn't tell if the look in his eyes was cold or peaceful. He led me out to deeper and deeper water as the waves crashed about us. We kissed, and he pressed my neck in a way that caused me to pass out. I lost my balance and went under water. He could have saved me, but he didn't.

This was a very dramatic and hard way to learn to

*not ever be a victim. I get it. And the flip side is to never
be a perpetrator. I get that, too. Amen.*

Again, I love you all.

Emily

_____Pearls of Wisdom

Several important themes stand out in these Transmissions. In both cases, they do not recommend revenge. Both murder victims want their surviving family members to live well, and if possible, turn the tragic experience into a way to help others. They implore their family members to not torment themselves with shame or blame, and to not live like a victim. Rather, they urge everyone to move forward and to fully enjoy the gift of life.

There is an additional important lesson from the second victim. She was forewarned and chose to ignore her inner knowing. Listening to others is important, but can get confusing. However, paying attention to what your body is telling you is a valuable asset and a helpful tool for navigating more effectively in life.

"You are driving yourself crazy and ruining your life over this, and that is not okay. I want you to heal and to talk about your experience. There are others who need to know how to recover from such a loss." –Julie

"The worst thing is to live your life focused on your own misery

and loss. It wears you down and paralyzes you, as you have noticed. All this self-torment does no one any good, and it certainly does not bother my killers." –Julie

"Revenge is not the path for you to take in relation to this crime and my death. Instead, please go out and talk to weak, hurting women in potentially violent relationships. Encourage them to put pride aside and to get help. Maybe just one woman will listen to the warning signs better than I was able, and it will save her life." –Emily

"Please love one another. Love yourselves. I love you. I feel loved right now in a way that I have never known." –Emily

"I preferred to believe lies and excuses and to overlook the obvious signs that this person was abusive to me. This was a very dramatic and hard way to learn to not ever be a victim." –Emily

___Why Wait Meditation: Receiving Guidance from Your Body

We all get feelings in our bodies when something, someone, a place, a relationship, or a decision does or does not feel right. The body has its own intelligence, which uses the language of sensations to let us know what's true and in our greatest good. Our bodies are talking to us all the time. Body signals do not lie. If someone you're talking with is saying all the right words, but does not mean them, your body will pick up the dissonance. Visceral reactions to people, job opportunities, physical spaces, and even daily choices are virtually instantaneous. The trick is to pay attention, to know what your body is trying to make you aware of, and to trust the message.

The mind is also an invaluable aspect of our overall intelligence; however, it can make up reasons to justify and rationalize anything, whether or not it is true or in our best interests. So when we have a body reaction to something/someone/situation and either ignore it altogether or ask the mind to make sense of it, what the mind figures out may or may not be true. Learning what your body is saying can save you time, energy, and heartache...perhaps even your life, if you choose to value it and to pay attention.

Simply put, the heart opens in the presence of positive energy, which signals the brain to release into the body the biochemistry of relaxation and well-being. Sometimes those sensations include a rush, shivers, relief, or even heart-opening tears.

The body automatically tightens and contracts when it encounters negative energy. The heart then signals the brain to activate the biochemistry of survival. This can include tensing muscles, sweating, jaw tightening, dry mouth, stomachache, or funny feeling.

Here is a three-part meditation to experience and become more aware of your body's messages.

PART ONE

○ *Close your eyes, and imagine you are sitting across from a person you know whom you truly like.*

○ *Stay with this experience for a couple of minutes so you can feel what goes on in your body when you imagine being in their positive presence.*

- *Remember how this feels and what it tells you as you encounter people and situations every day.*

PART TWO

- *Close your eyes, and imagine you are sitting across from a person you know and do not like.*

- *Stay with this experience long enough to notice how your body reacts to this person's energy.*

- *Remember how this feels and what it's telling you in everyday situations.*

PART THREE

- *When you are contemplating a new job, a move, or any personal decision, include a consult with your body's intelligence.*

- *Put aside all the pros and cons your mind is dishing up, and tune into your body.*

- *Sit quietly, close your eyes, and "try on" the job/the move/the relationship by imagining yourself in it, feeling what it's like to be doing it.*

- *You'll know if your body is offering you a green light or a red light...or even a yellow light saying you need more information before making a decision.*

Chapter 9

Transmissions from My Brother Jonathan Mann, MD

THIS BODY OF WORK began with the tragic deaths of my brother Jonathan, his wife, Mary Lou, and several hundred other people in the crash of Swissair Flight #111 in September 1998. Along with the sadness, which never fully goes away, his death continues to enrich my life in so many ways, including the opportunity to assist others by communicating with people who have died.

So, it is fitting to conclude this book by sharing more about his life, and to include this selection of additional Transmissions from my late brother.

About Jonathan Mann, MD

On a warm, summer evening in August of 1998, one month before the crash of Swissair #111, my brother Jonathan and I took a long walk together near his home in Virginia.

The moon had risen, the air was soft, and as Jonathan and I began to walk, he turned to me and said, "Carol, what do you think of when you hear the word virus?" I quickly replied, "A cold or a flu or something like that..." He paused. "That's the problem," he said. "I wish we hadn't called AIDS a virus because, like you, most people associate that word with a passing ailment, and AIDS is not a passing thing."

This kind of concern and self-reflection were typical of Jonathan. He would not have called himself a philosopher, but even as a child he was always deep in thought, pondering life, asking meaningful questions and searching for answers. I have two fond memories that exemplify this. One was at his Bar Mitzvah when Jonathan was thirteen; the other was when he was in high school.

In the traditional ceremony, the Rabbi offers a mini-sermon to the Bar Mitzvah boy. Typically, the boy listens politely, only possibly paying attention. In the middle of the sermon to my brother, the Rabbi posed a rhetorical question about the difference between the Tree of Life and The Tree of Knowledge. Not only had Jonathan been listening carefully, always the deep thinker, he spontaneously spoke up and offered a pithy answer. The Rabbi was surprised and impressed, and everyone burst out in spontaneous applause.

When he was in high school, Jonathan's favorite book was "The Plague," by Albert Camus. The main character, Dr. Rieux, devoted himself to helping people in the face of the seemingly unstoppable Plague. Dr. Rieux was one of Jonathan's heroes from that time forward. Somewhere in his soul, my brother must have known that this would become the model for his own life's work with the 21st century plague, HIV/AIDS.

His list of leadership roles, contributions, and accomplishments in slowing and resolving the global HIV/AIDS pandemic is enormous.

It was he who, in the 1980s, convinced the then-head of the World Health Organization that AIDS was a mounting global concern and that it was time to take action worldwide. As a result, Jonathan set up and led the WHO Program on Global AIDS.

Jonathan considered health and access to health care a Human Right. In his years of medical research, he observed that regardless of where HIV/AIDS began, it posed the greatest risk and spread most quickly among people who were already marginalized, stigmatized, and discriminated against. He discovered that loss of dignity is as much a predictor of disease as any germ.

Thus, he formulated his three-pronged approach to slowing and resolving the global spread of HIV/AIDS: education, biomedical research, and upgrading people's Human Rights.

He turned around discriminatory policies against people with AIDS in more than 150 countries, including ours. He participated in the establishment of World AIDS Day, inaugurated the first International Conference on HIV/AIDS to bring together scientists, human rights groups, health workers, doctors, educators, and people with HIV/AIDS. This unique, interdisciplinary gathering continues every year.

Jonathan created a new academic discipline called Health and Human Rights. He was the first Director of Harvard's Francois Bagnoud Center for Health and Human Rights, and the first Chair of Health and Human

Rights at the Harvard School of Public Health.

He wrote prolifically and spoke passionately as president of Doctors of the World. He held meetings with political leaders, health ministers, health workers, and AIDS patients all over the world.

With that long list of contributions, Jonathan talked about his work only if asked. He was a thoughtful person, kind, generous, and possessed a great sense of humor. We both spent teenage summers camping, hiking, and learning about nature in the Southwest. He continued his love for that part of the country and made time to visit its big skies and to hike its abundant trails. Each fall he'd gather ristras of hot chili peppers, which he froze and used over the winter months to make his favorite Tex-Mex meals. His latest kitchen adventure was making delicious, gourmet sorbets, which we sampled for dessert earlier that evening.

At the end of our walk together that full moon August night back in 1998, less than a month before the plane crash, Jonathan confided in me that what he most hoped for in his life was not about the list of what he had done...but to be and to be thought of...as a truly decent human being.

When people would ask him why he worked so tirelessly to change the world, his answer was, "If we don't try, will it ever change?"

*"Not only can I ask questions about anything
and get answers, but the response comes in
something like a movie...or actually a hologram,
like the Holodeck on* Star Trek.*"*
−Jonathan Mann

____Jonathan Tells Me More About the Afterlife

This was the second Transmission from my brother.

Dear Carol,

*The more I understand of how this new reality
works, the quicker it becomes less disorienting. You know
how I like to know where I am and how everything functions. Control freak, maybe?*

*My appearance is an example: Contained within the
"photo album" record of my experience is how I used to
look. In my current state, I can easily flip the "pages"
of my photo album, bringing to my awareness how I
looked at any age during my life. If I then focus on my
appearance at a specific age, it is like setting a favorite
station on your car radio; that image stays there. I have
been experimenting a little with this...getting my hair
free of grey, having a younger face and body, etc. I have
settled on me in my late thirties not looking like a kid,
but a younger and pleasing image to me.*

*To say that I am being instructed in the ways of this
new reality requires a different understanding of that
word. My experience is that this is a discovery process,
which seems to work in the following way. I am part
of a cohesive field of intelligence now, which includes
the greater collective and the information in my soul.*

Therefore, anything and everything can be known, at least to the degree I am evolved enough to formulate the questions and comprehend the responses.

As I pose questions, I draw an answer from the collective. I have no preoccupation (as I would have in my life) with whether or not this is the "right" answer. I know it to contain truth, and that's all that I need. If more information expands what I have previously learned, that's great. There is no resistance, no feeling or thoughts of, "Oh, I had it all wrong; this will upset my world."

Here are some more curious things. Not only can I ask questions about anything and get answers, but the response comes in something like a movie...or actually a hologram, like the Holodeck on Star Trek. *Therefore, I experience the answer fully; it registers with my complete set of perceptions.*

If I focus my attention on recalling a favorite place or person or event from my own life, this shows up like a hologram, too. If I think about how much I love hiking in the Southwest, it appears like I am actually there: walking, seeing, hearing, and feeling it in its fullness. If others are in this location or are also recalling this location, they appear in the scene as well. This seems to be a kind of time travel.

I have asked why it seems that I am (at least so far!) only recalling and drawing forth people and locations, which are beautiful, uplifting, and ennobling to me. What I understand is that the dominant feeling within a person when they die seems to set the stage for, at least, what comes pretty soon after death. The dominant feeling for me was love because I was with Mary Lou, and we were so grateful for each other. This final feeling tone has set in me a focus of bringing up positive recollections. I'll let you know if this continues.

Clearly, I can see that getting the gist of how focusing on something makes it show up, may be how, at some point, I might be given an assignment to do this rather than for my own personal pleasure. Haven't gotten there yet! Right now the challenge is mastering this, and it is totally consuming.

Love, Jonathan

___Questions to Jonathan

This is a series of questions, which Jonathan answered for me in Transmissions over the years.

CAROL: Are you with your wife?

JONATHAN: *The answer to this will not be a simple "yes" or "no." Since the crash, I really have not seen her in the way you are asking. I know she is recovering and being oriented, because here I have the ability to feel her presence at any time, and she can feel mine. Having the ability to connect with someone at any time is what makes the difference in not experiencing the "need" to see the person or having any anxiety about someone's absence. There is a constant experience of connectedness here. This is wonderful and creates a lot of inner peace for me. There is no need for phones or computers or wasting energy wondering how someone is or how they feel or what they are doing. Anytime I want to be with her, all I need to do is to think of her. So, I am with her all the time in that sense.*

I have come to realize that everyone is interconnected where you are, too. It is definitely possible for you to focus loving thoughts about someone in your heart and direct your consciousness to contact them. This is something you can practice. It feels really good and peaceful.

Had I been able to do this in any consistent way while I was alive, I would have been a much happier Earth camper. I guess it is obvious that all my preoccupations kept me in my head a great deal of the time.

CAROL: How are you feeling?

JONATHAN: *One of the things I am continuing to be amazed by is my lightness of being here. It is very pleasing, and not my former style, since you know I was a rather intense Type A person. What is new for me is discovering that it is possible to do what I consider meaningful, contributory things and still be very relaxed and light-hearted about it. I have no stress at all. Please share with people that stress and accomplishment are not required to go together.*

Here is another thing about living with a light-hearted approach, which is worth passing on to others. Happiness is not a state of being that anyone here tries to make happen. It is the byproduct of learning that most stress is self-created, and it is, therefore, optional. High-powered work does not have to mean high-powered stress.

This is not to say that everyone who is in a nonphysical state is happy and light. I can only speak of my experience. Maybe what is most true is that everyone here can have the benefit of help to let go of whatever ways they deprived themselves of happiness. There is a lot of assistance here to detach from our Earth-bound emotional traumas and dramas, which allows for so much more joy, and it is easier to do that here.

Regardless, there is no need to wait till you are on this side to experience the ecstasy of this kind of well-being. The less emotional baggage you carry around with you in life, the happier you will be. It is worth pursuing this, whatever it takes, and it usually takes forgiveness and letting go.

CAROL: Today would have been your birthday. I am wondering if that means anything to you where you are now?

JONATHAN: *Thanks for the loving thoughts of remembrance. Your feelings do reach me and flutter through me like a warm breeze. We do not have birthdays or holidays, but when you are directing your warm Happy Birthday thoughts my way, they create a pleasant sensation, which feels like someone is calling me. Another effect is that I am drawn (if I choose) into landscapes of birthday memories. I select happy ones if I decide to open that option.*

When large groups of people are celebrating holidays and are thinking positive thoughts of loved ones who are no longer with them, there is a huge, collective surge of love between your world and ours, which goes both ways.

CAROL: Are you able to travel to other locations? If so, how do you do that?

JONATHAN: *In this reality I can go anywhere my thoughts take me. So, I can think of being on the beach, and I am there. Or, I can think of being in your house, and I am there. The speed of thought is instantaneous, and so is the ability to create with thought. There is a lot of practice and skill to master this. You cannot have a single thought you don't really mean or want because it will manifest right in front of you. This cleans up any kind of old internal trash talk pretty fast…unless you like to experience chaos or to travel in circles!*

One clear benefit for me when I get rid of some of the internal mind chatter is that I can more easily communicate with you from our reality.

It's always worthwhile to clean out your thought closets for your own well-being while you are alive, too.

CAROL: Do you consider yourself to be "alive?"

JONATHAN: *I am very alive and in a broader context than imaginable. I have also mentioned that I am both part of a collective intelligence/consciousness field, and I have an individual "library" of experiences, the knowledge and wisdom in my soul. With hardly any "lock" onto the everyday reality of the physical world where you are, I have easy access to so much more.*

Your "alive" is limited to a particular way of perceiving. For example, where you are, reality is defined for most people by the five senses. (I know you and many others operate beyond those five as well.) So, what you can see, hear, taste, feel, and touch determines what is considered to be real and what is alive. You tend to define "life" as in a body, which looks a particular way, is breathing, requires oxygen, water, etc.

Pure consciousness does not require a body. And pure consciousness has the ability to interact with, and if required, to temporarily accommodate whatever form(s) a particular reality requires. From my perspective, everything in Creation is fed by pure consciousness and is alive. This is one of the most profound discoveries I have experienced.

CAROL: Do you have anything to say about the current state of HIV/AIDS in the world?

JONATHAN: *Only this: Things will change dramatically for the better in terms of global health and planetary wellness when everyone actively reveres every human being's life equally, and all resources are shared equally. The more you share love in all its forms, the more love there is to share. There is an unlimited supply.*

CAROL: I am curious to know what happens to our communication or even to our brother-sister relationship if/when you reincarnate on Earth?

JONATHAN: *A soul is an enormous concept and reality, and I don't pretend to understand it all yet. You are a soul, and you have a human body. You are a soul, and your soul expresses itself in different realities, in various time frames, in different forms and locations. The universe is huge and very full of life.*

All of this goes on simultaneously. However, realities can be experienced as separate, which allows the experience of being in only one place or one experience at a time. Remember the story that God puts a finger on every infant right above the lip (that little indent we all have), and with that, the baby forgets what came before?

The experience of forgetting who we are happens for most souls who have a body in the current, collective physical reality on Earth. The reality is structured in a way that makes it seem to be the only act in town. It also makes it seem that time is sequential. This works from the vantage point of your current Earth reality, but does not necessarily hold true elsewhere.

In some less-dense dimensions, it is possible to be fully aware of many of one's soul identities at once. I call the soul's many expressions "identity pods." Every soul has many, many identity pods, like so many cells in the mind of God. Where I am is less limited than your Earth reality, so it is possible to move the soul's consciousness (awareness) out of one pod and into another. It's also possible to create a new identity pod or to blend a few together in a new configuration. Souls are not limited by any physical reality and can move about with ease. In a certain sense, as souls, we are everywhere.

When wise teachers say that you are more than you realize, this is true.

Think of my recent life as your brother as one holographic book in the library, which makes up all the experiences housed in my soul. Anytime you want to contact that identity pod of mine, my soul is there for you in that persona and in that role. In this sense, you do not "lose" me when I reincarnate.

If you happen to meet my soul in a new body, you are personally sensitive enough to "recognize" my soul, and to relate to the new body and persona as who they are.

Assuming that is likely to happen between you and me while you are still alive, I would ask that you help the new version of me to remember some aspects of Jonathan so I can pick up where I left off. I hope to have grown in many ways and know I will still be challenged in others. I am pretty excited about the possibilities. I hope to come back with the ability to remember everything I currently know. As you may remember, I didn't like to waste time "growing up."

Sometime in the near future, the energy of the Earth herself will have accelerated enough, and bodies will also evolve to a higher frequency. At that time, it will not be necessary at all to spend between sixteen and twenty-one years growing up! That sounds great to me! How about you?

Love, Jonathan

___Pearls of Wisdom

Here are more pearls of wisdom and insightful information from this chapter of Transmissions from Jonathan.

"Not only can I ask questions about everything and get answers, but response comes in like a hologram, like the Holodeck on Star Trek. *Therefore, I experience the answer fully; it registers with my complete set of perceptions."*

"What is new for me is discovering that it is possible to do what I consider meaningful, contributory things and still be very relaxed and light-hearted about it. Please share with others that stress and accomplishment are not required to go together."

"When large groups of people are celebrating holidays and are thinking positive thoughts about loved ones no longer with them, there is a huge collective surge of love between your world and ours, which goes both ways."

"From my perspective, everything in Creation is fed by pure consciousness and is alive. This is one of the most profound discoveries I have experienced."

"...There is no need to wait till you are on this side to experience the ecstasy of this kind of well-being. The less emotional baggage you carry around with you in life, the happier you will be. It is worth pursuing this, whatever it takes, and it usually takes forgiveness and letting go."

_Why Wait Meditation: Feeling Forgiveness

Like all emotions, feelings of hurt, resentment, and anger are stored in the body until/unless they are released. Studies have shown that holding grudges causes negative physiological and emotional effects, including literally contracting the heart and other vessels, impairing the immune system, and elevating blood pressure.

Research has shown that the inability to forgive is a significant predictor of major illness. Therefore, carrying a grudge is like "condo-sharing" with the perpetrator in your body. He or she is fine and off living their life. On the other hand, you are forever carrying the toxin.

Forgiveness is not about condoning painful events, nor is it about letting someone else off the hook. It is about releasing the constrictions in your body, which come from holding onto resentments, hurts, and grudges.

Here is a simple meditation that will allow you to experience what forgiveness feels like in the body, as well as a preview of how freeing it is to forgive.

- *Find a comfortable place to sit where you will not be interrupted for ten minutes.*

- *Close your eyes, and take three deep breaths. Bring your awareness to your physical heart and imagine you can inhale and exhale through your own heart.*

- *Continue to breathe in and out of your heart like this for several minutes.*

- *Now, try on the feeling of forgiveness without any content, just the feeling.*

- *Notice how your body feels.*

- *Gently open your eyes.*

Chapter 10

Conversations with Lea: A Rare Opportunity

SINCE I HARDLY USE my landline anymore, I often don't think to check to see if I have any messages on that old answering machine, but as I walked into my house one late evening this past June, I couldn't miss seeing the telltale red message light blinking away in the dark kitchen. I had just come home from the second-to-last meeting of a writer's group I had joined to help support me in writing this book.

I flipped on the kitchen light, quickly let my excited dogs run through my legs and out the door to get rid of pent-up energy from being inside all evening and began to listen. There on the machine was the very clear, soft-spoken and familiar voice of a dear woman named Lea, whom I had not heard from in almost ten years. In her gentle, matter-of-fact tone she said she was dying of cancer and hoped to talk with me. Would I please call her back?

When I returned Lea's call, and she told me her story, it became clear that hers would be the final chapter in this book. She wanted to talk about how she was consciously experiencing bridging two realities, her everyday life and life on the other side. Talking with her, I knew that here was someone smart and self-aware, who could share some glimpses into what it is like after death while still alive in this world.

The synchronicity of her call and writing this book did not escape me. In fact, goosebumps made the hairs on my arms stand on end. I had done a Soul Reading for Lea and some coaching for her a long time ago, and over the years she had come to several workshops I facilitated around the country.

We agreed to a series of phone conversations in which I would essentially interview her. Naturally, I told her about her impeccable and very cosmic timing in terms of my writing project, and asked if I might share her insights. She was delighted and with great excitement exclaimed, "Oh, if only everyone could live their lives knowing what I know now!"

I recorded three separate, hour-long conversations over the next couple of months. The next pages are taken directly from our conversations.

May we all have the grace to live our dying with such expanded awareness, presence, and inner peace.

_____My Interview with Lea – Summer of 2011

Lea is in her early sixties. She has several grown children and has devoted her work to advocating for people faced with navigating our legal system. Most recently, she has been a college professor. As you will see, Lea is self-aware, honest, and courageous.

CAROL: Neither of us are strangers to the fact that life's challenges often include opportunities for major personal growth. Do you have any special insights that have come to you during this difficult time?

LEA: *The biggest gift to me in this cancer is a profound sense of connection with all of humanity. My own life has not been difficult, and I thought I would be exempt from cancer. Now I am facing my death, which makes me totally aware that I am part of this long, unbroken chain of human living and dying. For the first time in my life, I feel camaraderie with all of humanity. This is very comforting; it gives me a very deep experience of communion with life.*

CAROL: Forgive me for being so direct; I would like to ask about the status of your illness and how you are spending your days now?

LEA: *This illness is progressing, and it is inoperable. Really, I have a tumor under my ribs, which is the size of Rhode Island! I don't look the same. I look like a corpse, but I just let it go and be where I am. I am fully present, regardless of what the corpse photo on my new driver's license reveals. I am fully alive, no matter the state of my body. I just get up each day and live my life. People comment on my voice; it is strong.*

I have seen the tumor with my inner vision and have even dialogued with it. For example, it has never told me that it is going away. My body is failing. I can feel it speeding up. For example, lately, I am aware that my kidneys are slowing down and are overwhelmed by this tumor.

CAROL: Are you in pain?

LEA: *One night when I came back from work, I did have some pain, so I asked the tumor to stop the hurt, and it said back to me, "I'll stop when you stop trying to please everyone." That was both funny and true. This is not about doom and gloom. I just know that slowly and surely it will take my life, BUT not my light.*

It is quite an amazing phenomenon that I am not in pain, so I am not at all consumed with trying to ease any sort of physical discomfort. I am therefore not anchored by pain to this physical world. Being mostly pain-free is allowing me to experience things beyond this physical reality, for which I am grateful. It is obvious to me that I am no longer limited by operating in linear time, clock time, or calendar time.

CAROL: You just said that you are now aware of things beyond this reality. Can you say more, please?

LEA: *I am experiencing all that I am telling you, not because I am psychic: It is because I am no longer locked in to time the way most people are in their worldly lives. Here are some examples of phenomena occurring now, which I have not experienced previously in my life.*

In my current state of being here and not here, I have the uncanny ability to immediately see into the psyche of everyone I encounter, even strangers. If a person is talking about any topic, I know where that thread of conversation and feeling goes for them. It is usually more information than I want. I am way ahead of them in terms of what I know they are going to say and what they are actually sharing in the moment.

So, if this happens when I am in a conversation, I just wait for the person to catch up with where I already know they are going. There would be no more secrets if everyone could function like this in nonlinear time. No more secrets would be a good thing for the world.

CAROL: I would enjoy that, I think! Are you also able to see or predict other things about people?

LEA: *Yes, sometimes I also know things about people before they occur in "real time." I can see what people have cast into their future, and what they will play out.*

From my new vantage point, there seems to be a finite number of human story patterns with predictable outcomes. Here is my insight: Our destiny paths are precast by us. Everyone's story depends on how we interpret the events life brings to us. Another way to say this, which is not original to me, is that it's not what happens to us in life, but what meaning we give it, that makes all the difference. Once we have created a story, everything feeds it, and there are predictable life patterns and outcomes, which go with that story.

Here's the good news: I can also see now that these outcomes are ultimately optional. So, I say to myself and to you, what do you want to construct for yourself? What story are you placing yourself in and being run by? The three big roles in life that I notice people get stuck in are victim, perpetrator, and rescuer. These three are important to step away from. All this is flexible and fixable if you want, but you have to be able to see what you are creating first.

CAROL: This is great information for everyone to seriously consider and to act on. Is there more?

LEA: *Oh, I also know in advance when things are not going to happen. For example, when I hear a given weather forecast, I know if it will or won't play out that way. Here's another example:*

If someone says they'll stop by for a visit, I know if they are not going to show up. This is really nice; I don't even bother preparing.

These examples may seem very mundane, but if we can tell what is and what is not going to happen, we have a new and freeing way to navigate in our lives. It makes things so much more efficient, with no more wasted energy. Keep in mind that my new perceptions have everything to do with having less of a grip on time and more of an opening to my soul. This means that everyone has this ability, and you don't need to be dying to expand what's possible.

CAROL: Can you explain how you know everything you are now able to perceive?

LEA: *All that I have shared about seeing what people are casting for their destinies, and what will and will not come to pass, happens to me as direct knowing. What I mean is that there is nothing between me and the answer. Everyone has this experience from time to time where you just know things. I am having it more often, which is another new and wonderful gift from my spirit.*

CAROL: I love how you are relating to these new abilities as gifts from your spirit. Okay, so I have a hunch you have more wisdom to share right now.

LEA: *Here is something else, which means a lot to me. I am simultaneously experiencing a very big picture of life and the little one here in this Earth reality. Seeing the big picture has taken away my old fears and issues. I didn't do anything for that to happen. It is part of the territory of being in the big picture. In that larger view, I experience that my life has no beginning and no end. In the little picture, the end is already here.*

The loss of my physical body is not a significant event in my big-picture life; it doesn't touch me. There is a great deal of sentimentality that most people project onto life and death here.

This interferes with the bigger truth, and makes things much more painful.

CAROL: Speaking of pain, how do you cope with setbacks in your illness?

LEA: *I do have physical setbacks, which get my attention in both the smaller view of my life and the larger picture. Like, I lose my balance and fall a lot. Thankfully, I have not seriously hurt myself, but my body boundaries are disappearing. I fall when I don't know where my legs are. Lying on the floor after a tumble, I say to myself, "Uh oh, maybe this will be harder than I think," and I get a bit scared.*

But quickly, that larger consciousness of mine takes over and becomes the observer of all this. I take stock of the situation and then the whole process becomes very fascinating. As the observer of all that's going on, I return to that knowing state. I don't create a story to get freaked out about like, "Oh my God, I just fell, what am I going to do?" Without a drama story, I have nothing to react to or to attach to; and therefore, it just is what it is. My clarity is restored, and I take care of my body without any story, and I am fine again.

CAROL: Other people have spoken to me about bridging the realities between here and the other side and communicating with their spirit guides. Has anything like this happened for you?

LEA: *Not exactly, but here is another and very unexpected source of comfort for me, in addition, of course, to friends, family, and healers. There is a man whom I once knew when I was a child and my family lived abroad. I have not had any contact with him for all these decades. In "real time," he is now elderly, and like me, is in the process of dying.*

How do I know this? Every now and then he pops into my

awareness. I see him with my eyes open and communicate with him using telepathy. He is accompanying me in this journey of transition.

He checks in on me, and even though he is old and ill, his cheery and periodic presence is very comforting. This is not a hallucination; it is part of my expanded awareness. People can find each other on the Internet, but we can also do the same thing with our consciousness!

CAROL: I am so humbled and grateful to you, Lea, for sharing all this with me and with those who will read this book. It is such an honor to bear witness to your process and to benefit from your experience. Is there anything you would you like to say to conclude our interview?

LEA: *Thank you for this opportunity. I hope it helps others. I don't know how long I'll be here, and I know now that it does not matter. I already have the demonstration that my consciousness goes way beyond my body because I am in a skeletal body having so much awareness. This may not make any medical sense, but my consciousness is more all-knowing than ever, as simultaneously, my body is falling apart.*

I feel like I will just be trading places; my consciousness will become more and more dominant, and my physical body will become less and less functional. I know that I am the consciousness animating this body and, simultaneously, experiencing things way beyond. I experience the fact of operating in at least two realities. It is so reassuring that there is so much more. I am very happy and very peaceful.

Meanwhile, I just keep getting up each day and living my life. I am right at the edge of seeing that this small picture of life is just an illusion. My experience is that I am on the other side of the veil, even when I am still doing the mundane things in my life. I am not ready to give up my body yet, and at the same time, I can feel that there will be a time when I will know to tell it goodbye.

When I do actually transition, well that will have been me living in that life, and I will be curious to discover and fully experience my soul in other realities. I am very relaxed about all of this, and I will leave with a grateful heart.

Lea passed away right after the New Year in 2012.

> *"And did you get what you wanted from this life, even so?*
> *I did.*
> *And what did you want?*
> *To call myself beloved, to feel myself beloved on the Earth."*

−from *Late Fragment,* Lea's favorite poem by Raymond Carver, provided to me by Lea's sister

_Afterword

WISE TEACHERS HAVE ALWAYS said that separation is an illusion. This is a hard concept to grasp and even more difficult to feel—living in the limitations of our current dualistic reality, where we experience such loss and grieve so deeply when someone dies.

However, the end of the illusion of separation is at hand. Science is now bringing us the evidence, which ancient mystical teachings also honor, that all life in the universe is one interactive and interconnected phenomenon. There is data from quantum physics revealing that everything is in constant communication with everything in creation, space is not empty, and all of creation is one linked-in, living, evolving phenomenon.

Therefore, there is no true separation, only the beliefs, which have until now, kept us limited. The human brain will actually censor data, which challenges a strongly held belief. For example, the world has always been a sphere, even when people believed it was flat. However, that collective belief screened out any other possibilities, and people feared they might fall off the edge and die if they went too far. Did they collectively believe the world was flat? Yes. Was that true? No. Did what they believe and the fear they generated make it seem absolutely true? Yes.

We are now at another new frontier, where the old belief about separation may not be real. Imagine the possibilities in our Earthly lives when we can be consciously aware of the love and wisdom from souls who are no longer in this physical reality. Think how humanity as a whole can benefit and evolve from learning what those on the other side know and can perceive... and when we know that dying is not the end, how might that change how we live?

As you have read in this book, souls on the other side are a part of the human family who desire inclusion in our lives. They are doing their best to actively contribute to us, even when we cannot yet fully perceive their presence.

Now it is our turn to purposely revisit what is possible and to actually let go of what we think we know in order to remove the long-standing veils between realities.

My late father was a physician and an innovator, whose contributions in his field advanced the practice of psychiatry. In a recent Transmission from the other side, my father reminded me of the following...as I now remind us all in closing:

The nature of life is that it is always expressing itself through new points of view and revealing new possibilities. Somehow, the ultimate life skill is to hold beliefs as only a temporary foundation of truth. There is always more. Being stuck in outdated beliefs locks you in and leaves you locked out of infinite possible discoveries and pleasures.

James Mann, MD

To enjoy your greatest fulfillment here and now, I invite you to repeat the following to yourself often as you walk through life: "With my open human heart, I choose love."

_Acknowledgments

I am deeply grateful to all my friends and clients who support my work and whose lives, loves, and losses enrich my life immeasurably:

- To my dear friend Laury, who "got it" about this book and designed such a perfect cover,

- To my "book angel," Becky Benenate, for her kindness and professional guidance,

- To my daughter, Ariel, who has always been my most treasured fan.

For more information about current seminars,
personal Soul Readings or Transmissions of loved
ones who have passed, please visit:
www.yourcosmiccafe.com

Carol Mann also hosts a radio show called Cosmic Café.
Recordings of her shows are available at:
www.yourcosmiccafe.com